Ancient Manuscripts
of the Freemasons

The Transformation from
Operative to Speculative Freemasonry

Edited by Michael R. Poll

Ancient Manuscripts of the Freemasons
Edited by Michael R. Poll

A Cornerstone Book
Published by Cornerstone Book Publishers
An Imprint of Michael Poll Publishing
Copyright © 2009-2023 by Cornerstone Book Publishers

All rights reserved under International and Pan-American Copyright Conventions. No part of this book may be reproduced in any manner without permission in writing from the copyright holder, except by a reviewer, who may quote brief passages in a review.

Cornerstone Book Publishers
Hot Springs, AR

First Cornerstone Edition - 2009
Second Cornerstone Edition - 2011
Third Cornerstone Edition - 2013
Fourth Cornerstone Edition – 2014
Fifth Cornerstone Edition - 2023

www.cornerstonepublishers.com

Foreword

In our search for a better understanding of the history of Freemasonry, few collections are more relevant than these presented in this book. Included here are some of the most significant documents tracing Freemasonry from its early Operative years to the seeds of Speculative Freemasonry.

The Operative Freemasons organized themselves into lodges, apprentices were instructed by masters, and from all were required obligations and following rules of conduct not so far removed from what we know today in our Speculative Freemasonry. Certainly, the exact words and particular customs have changed over time, but a study of these old manuscripts shows us a recognizable form of Freemasonry. It is from these early lodges (directly or through inspiration) that we grew and evolved into the Freemasonry we know today.

The goal of this book is to present the Masonic student with a convenient collection of these rare and important Masonic manuscripts to complement his present Masonic education program. It is hoped that this collection will whet your appetite for deeper study into the philosophy and history of Freemasonry.

This collection is presented as a study aid. In some cases, the original text is provided along with the more modern text. In other cases, only the more modern text. The hope is that, while this should not be taken to be the exact original texts in all cases, the flavor and idea of the manuscripts are presented.

Michael R. Poll
October 2009

Table of Contents

Foreword iii
The Old Charges of Freemasonry 1
Freemasonry And The Comacine Masters 13
Edict of Rothari 25
Regius Manuscript (Modern Text) 27
Regius Manuscript (Original Text) 52
The Matthew Cooke Manuscript 78
The Torgau Ordinances 92
The Strasburg Manuscript 106
Watson Manuscript 119
The Schaw Statutes (First) 129
The Schaw Statutes (Second) 133
St. Clair Charters 136
Harleian Manuscript 141
Sloane Ms. No. 3848 143
Inigo Jones Manuscript 151
Thomas Tew Manuscript 162
Edinburgh Register House Manuscript 164
Sloane Ms. No. 3329 168
The Kevan Manuscript 173
Robert's Constitutions 177
Ancient Charges of a FREE MASON (1723) 188
General Regulations of a Freemason 195
The Graham Manuscript 207
Ancient Charges of a FREE MASON (1738) 208

Ancient Manuscripts
of the Freemasons

The Old Charges of Freemasonry
By H. L. Haywood
The Builder, September 1923

What the Old Charges Are

I have just come from reading an article in one of the more obscure masonic periodicals in which an unknown brother lets go with this very familiar remark: "As for me, I am not interested in the musty old documents of the past. I want to know what is going on today." The context makes it clear that he had in mind the Old Charges. A sufficient reply to this ignoramus is that the Old Charges are among the things that are "going on today." Eliminate them from Freemasonry as it now functions and not a subordinate lodge, or a Grand Lodge, or any other regular masonic body could operate at all; they are to what the Constitution of this nation is to the United States government, and what its statutes are to every state in the Union. All our constitutions, statutes, laws, rules, by-laws and regulations to some extent or other hark back to the Old Charges, and without them masonic jurisprudence, or the methods for governing and regulating the legal affairs of the Craft, would be left hanging suspended in the air. In proportion as masonic leaders, Grand Masters, Worshipful Masters and Jurisprudence Committees ignore, or forget, or misunderstand these masonic charters they run amuck, and lead the Craft into all manner of wild and unmasonic undertakings. If some magician could devise a method whereby a clear conception of the Old Charges and what they stand for could be installed into the head of every active mason in the land, it would save us all from embarrassment times without number and it would relieve Grand Lodges and other Grand bodies from the needless expenditure of hundreds of thousands of dollars every year. If there is any practical necessity, any hard down-next-to-the-ground necessity anywhere in Freemasonry today, it is for a general clear-headed understanding of the Ancient Constitutions and landmarks of our Order.

By the OLD CHARGES is meant those ancient documents that have come down to us from the fourteenth century and afterwards in which are incorporated the traditional history, the legends and the rules and regulations of Freemasonry. They are called variously "Ancient Manuscripts", "Ancient Constitutions", "Legend of the Craft", "Gothic Manuscripts", "Old Records", etc, etc. In their physical makeup these documents are sometimes found in the form of handwritten paper or parchment rolls, the units of which are either sewn or pasted together; of hand-written sheets stitched together in book form, and in the familiar printed form of a modern book. Sometimes they are found incorporated in the minute book of a lodge. They range in estimated date from 1390 until the first quarter of the eighteenth century, and a few of them are specimens of beautiful Gothic script. The largest number of them are in the keeping of the British Museum; the masonic library of West Yorkshire, England, has in custody the second largest number.

As already said these Old Charges (such is their most familiar appellation) form the basis of modern masonic constitutions, and therefore jurisprudence. They establish the continuity of the masonic institution through a period of more than five centuries, and by fair implication much longer; and at the same time, and by token of the same significance, prove the great antiquity of Masonry by written documents, which is a thing no other craft in existence is able to do. These manuscripts are traditional and legendary in form and are therefore not to be read as histories are, nevertheless a careful and critical study of them based on internal evidence sheds more light on the earliest times of Freemasonry than any other one source whatever. It is believed that the Old Charges were used in making a Mason in the old Operative days; that they served as constitutions of lodges in many cases, and sometimes functioned as what we today call a warrant.

The systematic study of these manuscripts began in the middle of the past century, at which time only a few were known to be in existence. In 1872 William James Hughan listed 32. Owing largely to his efforts many others were discovered, so that in 1889 Gould was able to list 62, and Hughan himself in 1895 tabulated 66 manuscript copies, 9 printed versions and 11 missing versions. This number has been so much increased of late years that in *Ars Quatuor Coronatorum, Volume XXXI*, page 40 (1918), Brother Roderick H. Baxter, now Worshipful Master of Quatuor Coronati Lodge, listed 98, which number included the versions known to be missing. Brother Baxter's

list is peculiarly valuable in that he gives data as to when and where these manuscripts have been reproduced.

For the sake of being better able to compare one copy with another, Dr. W. Begemann classified all the versions into four general "families", The Grand Lodge Family, The Sloane Family, The Roberts Family, and The Spencer Family. These family groups he divided further into branches, and he believed that The Spencer Family was an offshoot of The Grand Lodge Family, and The Roberts Family an offshoot of The Sloane Family. In this general manner of grouping, the erudite doctor was followed by Hughan, Gould and their colleagues, and his classification still holds in general; attempts have been made in recent years to upset it, but without much success. One of the best charts, based on Begemann, is that made by Brother Lionel Vibert, a copy of which will be published in a future issue of The Builder.

The first known printed reference to these Old Charges was made by Dr. Robert Plot in his Natural History of Staffordshire, published in 1686. Dr. A.F.A. Woodford and William James Hughan were the first to undertake a scientific study. Hughan's Old Charges is to this day the standard work in English. Gould's chapter in his History of Masonry would probably be ranked second in value, whereas the voluminous writings of Dr. Begemann, contributed by him to Zirkelcorrespondez, official organ of the National Grand Lodge of Germany, would, if only they were translated into English, give us the most exhaustive treatment of the subject ever yet written.

The Old Charges are peculiarly English. No such documents have ever been found in Ireland. Scotch manuscripts are known to be of English origin. It was once held by Findel and other German writers that the English versions ultimately derived from German sources, but this has been disproved. The only known point of similarity between the Old Charges and such German documents as the Torgau Ordinances and the Cologne Constitutions is the Legend of the Four Crowned Martyrs, and this legend is found among English versions only in the Regius Manuscript. As Gould well says, the British MSS. have "neither predecessors nor rivals"; they are the richest and rarest things in the whole field of masonic writings.

When the Old Charges are placed side by side it is immediately seen that in their account of the traditional history of the Craft they vary in a great many particulars, nevertheless they appear to have derived from some common origin, and in the main they tell the same tale, which is as interesting as a fairy story out of Grimm. Did the original of this traditional account come from some individual or was it born out of a floating tradition, like the folk tales of ancient people? Authorities differ much on this point. Begemann not only declared that the first version of the story originated with an individual, but even set out what he deemed to be the literary sources used by that Great Unknown. The doctor's arguments are powerful. On the other hand, others contend that the story began as a general vague oral tradition, and that this was in the course of time reduced to writing. In either event, why was the story ever written? In all probability an answer to that question will never be forth-coming, but W. Harry Rylands and others have been of the opinion that the first written versions were made in response to a general Writ for Return issued in 1388. Rylands' words may be quoted: "It appears to me not at all improbable that much, if not all, of the legendary history was composed in answer to the Writ for Returns issued to the guilds all over the country, in the twelfth year of Richard the Second, A.D. 1388." (A.Q.C. XVL page 1)

II. The Two Oldest Manuscripts

In 1757 King George II presented to the British Museum a collection of some 12,000 volumes, the nucleus of which had been laid by King Henry VII and which came to be known as the Royal Library. Among these books was a rarely beautiful manuscript written by hand on 64 pages of vellum, about four by five inches in size, which a cataloger, David Casley, entered as No. 17 A-1 under the title, "A Poem of Moral Duties: here entitled Constitutiones Artis Gemetrie Secundem." It was not until Mr. J.O. Halliwell, F.R.S. (afterwards Halliwell-Phillipps), a non-Mason, chanced to make the discovery that the manuscript was known to be a masonic document. Mr. Phillipps read a paper on the manuscript before the Society of Antiquaries in 1839, and in the following year published a volume entitled Early History of Freemasonry in England (enlarged and revised in 1844), in which he incorporated a transcript of the document along with a few pages in facsimile. This important work will be found incorporated in the familiar Universal Masonic Library, the rusty sheepskin bindings of which strike the eyes on almost every masonic book shelf. This manuscript was known as "The Halliwell", or as "The Halliwell-Phillipps" until some fifty years atfterwards Gould rechristened it, in honour of the Royal Library in which it is found, the "Regius", and since then this has become the more familiar cognomen.

David Casley, a learned specialist in old manuscripts, dated the "Regius" as of the fourteenth century. E.A. Bond, another expert, dated it as of the middle of the fifteenth century. Dr. Kloss, the German specialist, placed it between 1427 and 1445. But the majority have agreed on 1390 as the most probable date. "It is impossible to arrive at absolute certainty on this point," says Hughan, whose Old Charges should be consulted, "save that it is not likely to be older than 1390, but may be some twenty years or so later." Dr. W. Begemann made a study of the document that has never been equalled for thoroughness, and arrived at a conclusion that may be given in his own words: it was written "towards the end of the 14th or at least quite at the beginning of the 15th century (not in Gloucester itself, as being too southerly, but) in the north of Gloucestershire or in the neighbouring north of Herefordshire, or even possibly in the south of Worcestershire." (A.Q.C. VII, page 35.)

In 1889 an exact facsimile of this famous manuscript was published in Volume I of the *Antigrapha* produced by the Quatuor Coronati Lodge of Research, and was edited by the then secretary of that lodge, George William Speth, himself a brilliant authority, who supplied a glossary that is indispensable to the amateur student. Along with it was published a commentary by R. F. Gould, one of the greatest of all his masonic papers, though it is exasperating in its rambling arrangement and general lack of conclusiveness.

The Regius Manuscript is the only one of all the versions to be written in meter, and may have been composed by a priest, if one may judge by certain internal evidences, though the point is disputed. There are some 800 lines in the poem, the strictly masonic portion coming to an end at line 576, after which begins what Hughan calls a "sermonette" on moral duties, in which there is quite a Roman

Catholic vein with references to "the sins seven", "the sweet lady" (referring to the Virgin) and to holy water. There is no such specific Mariolatry in any other version of the Old Charges, though the great majority of them express loyalty to "Holy Church" and all of them, until Anderson's familiar version, are specifically Christian, so far as religion is concerned.

The author furnishes a list of fifteen "points" and fifteen "articles", all of which are quite specific instructions concerning the behaviour of a Craftsman: this portion is believed by many to have been the charges to an initiate as used in the author's period, and is therefore deemed the most important feature of the book as furnishing us a picture of the regulations of the Craft at that remote date. The Craft is described as having come into existence as an organized fraternity in "King Adelstoune's day", but in this the author contradicts himself, because he refers to things "written in old books" (I modernize spelling of quotations) and takes for granted a certain antiquity for the Masonry, which, as in all the Old Charges, is made synonymous with Geometry, a thing very different in those days from the abstract science over which we laboured during our school days.

The Regius Poem is evidently a book about Masonry, rather than a document of Masonry, and may very well have been written by a non-mason, though there is no way in which we can verify such theories, especially seeing that we know nothing about the document save what it has to tell us about itself, which is little.

In his Commentary on the Regius MS, R. F. Gould produced a paragraph that has ever since served as the pivot of a great debate. It reads as follows and refers to the "sermonette" portion which deals with "moral duties": "These rules of decorum read very curiously in the present age, but their inapplicability to the circumstances of the working masons of the fourteen or fifteenth century will be at once apparent. They were intended for the gentlemen of those days, and the instruction for behaviour in the presence of a lord-at table and in the society of ladies-would have all been equally out of place in a code of manners drawn up for the use of a Guild or Craft of Artisans."

The point of this is that there must have been present among the Craftsmen of that time a number of men not engaged at all in labour, and therefore were, as we would now describe them, "speculatives."

This would be of immense importance if Gould had made good his point, but that he was not able to do. The greatest minds of the period in question were devoted to architecture, and there is no reason not to believe that among the Craftsmen were members of good families. Also the Craft was in contact with the clergy all the while, and therefore many of its members may well have stood in need of rules for preserving proper decorum in great houses and among the members of the upper classes. From Woodford until the present time the great majority of masonic scholars have believed the Old Charges to have been used by a strictly operative craft and it is evident that they will continue to do so until more conclusive evidence to the contrary is forthcoming than Gould's surmise.

Next to the Regius the oldest manuscript is that known as the Cooke. It was published by R. Spencer, London, 1861 and was edited by Mr. Matthew Cooke, hence his name. In the British Museum's catalogue it is listed as "Additional M.S. 23,198", and has been dated by Hughan at 1450 or thereabouts, an estimate in which most of the specialists have concurred. Dr. Begemann believed the document to have been "compiled and written in the southeastern portion of the western Midlands, say, in Gloucestershire or Oxfordshire, possibly also in southeast Worcestershire or southwest Warwickshire. The 'Book of Charges' which forms the second part of the document is certainly of the 14th century, the historical or first part, of quite the beginning of the 15th." (A.Q.C. IX, page 18)

The Cooke MS. was most certainly in the hands of Mr. George Payne, when in his second term as Grand Master in 1720 he compiled the "General Regulations", and which Anderson included in his own version of the Constitutions published in 1723. Anderson himself evidently made use of lines 901-960 of the MS.

The Lodge Quatuor Coronati reprinted the Cooke in facsimile in Vol. II of its Antigrapha in 1890, and included therewith a Commentary by George William Speth which is, in my own amateur opinion, an even more brilliant piece of work than Gould's Commentary on the Regius. Some of Speth's conclusions are of permanent value. I paraphrase his findings in my own words:

The M.S. is a transcript of a yet older document and was written by a mason. There were several versions of the Charges to a Mason in circulation at the time. The MS. is in two parts, the former of which is an attempt at a history of the Craft, the latter of which is a version of the Charges. Of this portion Speth writes that it is "far and away the earliest, best and purest version of the 'Old Charges' which we possess." The MS. mentions nine "articles", and these evidently were legal enforcements at the time; the nine "points" given were probably not legally binding but were morally so. "Congregations" of Masons were held here and there but no "General Assembly" (or "Grand Lodge"); Grand Masters existed in fact but not in name and presided at one meeting of a congregation only. "Many of our present usages may be traced in their original form to this manuscript."

III. Anderson's Constitutions and Other Printed Versions

One of the most important of all the versions of the Old Charges is not an ancient original at all, but a printed edition issued in 1722, and known as the Roberts, though it is believed to be a copy of an ancient document. Of this W. J. Hughan writes: "The only copy known was purchased by me at Brother Spencer's sale of masonic works, etc. (London, 1875), for 8 pounds 10s., on behalf of the late Brother R. F. Bower, and is now in the magnificent library of the Grand Lodge of Iowa, U.S.A." This tiny volume is easily the most priceless masonic literary possession in America, and was published in exact facsimile by the National masonic Research Society, with an eloquent Introduction by Dr. Joseph Fort Newton in 1916. The Reverend Edmund Coxe edited a famous reprint in 1871. It is a version meriting the most careful study on the part of the masonic student because it had a decided influence on the literature and jurisprudence of the Craft after its initial appearance. It appeared in one of the most interesting and momentous periods of modern Speculative Masonry, namely, in the years between the organization of the first Grand Lodge in 1717 and the appearance of Anderson's Constitution in 1723. It is the earliest printed version of the Old Charges known to exist.

Another well-known printed version is that published in 1724 and known as the Briscoe. This was the second publication of its kind. The third printed version was issued in 1728-9 by Benjamin Cole, and known as the Cole Edition in consequence. This version is considered a literary gem in that the main body of the text is engraved throughout in most beautiful style. A special edition of this book was made in Leeds, 1897, the value of which was enhanced by one of W. J. Hughan's famous introductions. For our own modern and practical purposes the most important of all the versions ever made was that compiled by Dr. James Anderson in 1723 and everywhere known familiarly as Anderson's Constitution. A second edition appeared, much changed and enlarged, in 1738; a third, by John Entick, in 1756; and so on every few years until by 1888 twenty-two editions in all had been issued. The Rev. A.F.A. Woodford, Hughan's collaborator, edited an edition of The Constitution Book of 1723 as Volume I of Kenning's masonic Archeological Library, under date of 1878. This is a correct and detailed reproduction of the book exactly as Anderson first published it, and is valuable accordingly.

Anderson's title page is interesting to read: "The CONSTITUTION, History, Laws, Charges, Orders, Regulations, and Usages, of the Right Worshipful FRATERNITY of ACCEPTED FREE MASONS; collected from their general RECORDS, and their faithful TRADITIONS of many Ages. To be read At the Admission of a NEW BROTHER, when the Master or Warden shall begin, or order some other Brother to read as follows, etc." After the word "follows" Anderson's own version of masonic history begins with this astonishing statement:

"Adam, our first Parent, created after the Image of God, the great Architect of the Universe, must have had the Liberal Sciences, particularly Geometry, written on his Heart, etc."

Thus did Dr. Anderson launch his now thrice familiar account of the history of Freemasonry, an account which, save in the hands of the most expert masonic antiquarian, yields very little dependable historical fact whatsoever, but which, owing to the prestige of its author, came to be accepted for generations as a bona fide history of the Craft. It will be many a long year yet before the rank and file of brethren shall have learned that Dr. Anderson's "history" belongs in the realm of fable for the most part, and has never been accepted as anything else by knowing ones.

The established facts concerning Dr. Anderson's own private history comprise a record almost as brief as the short and simple annals of the poor. Brother J.T. Thorp, one of the most distinguished of the veterans among living English masonic scholars, has given it in an excellent brief form. (A.Q.C. XVIII, page 9.)

"Of this distinguished Brother we know very little. He is believed to have been born, educated and made a Mason in Scotland, subsequently settling in London as a Presbyterian Minister. He is mentioned for the first time in the Proceedings of the Grand Lodge of England on September 29th, 1721, when he was appointed to revise the old Gothic Constitutions-this revision was approved by the Grand Lodge of England on September 29th in 1723, in which year Anderson was Junior Grand Warden under the Duke of Wharton-he published a second edition of the Book of Constitutions in 1738, and died in 1739. This is about all that is known of him."

In his 1738 edition Anderson so garbled up his account of the founding of Grand Lodge, and contradicted his own earlier story in such fashion, that R. F. Gould was inclined to believe either that he had become disgruntled and full of spleen, or else that he was in his dotage. Be that as it may, Anderson's historical pages are to be read with extreme caution. His Constitution itself, or that part dealing with the principles and regulations of the Craft, is most certainly a compilation made of extracts of other versions of the Old Charges pretty much mixed with the Doctor's own ideas in the premises, and so much at variance with previous customs that the official adoption thereof caused much dissension among the lodges, and may have had something to do with the disaffection which at last led to the formation of the "Antient" Grand Lodge of 1751 or thereabouts. The "Anderson" of this latter body, which in time waxed very powerful, was Laurence Dermott, a brilliant Irishman, who as Grand Secretary was leader of the "Antient" forces for many years, and who wrote for the body its own Constitution, called Ahiman Rezon, which cryptic title is believed by some to mean "Worthy Brother Secretary." The first edition of this important version was made in 1756, a second in 1764, and so on until by 1813 an eighth had been published. A very complete collection of all editions is in the masonic Library at Philadelphia. A few of our Grand Lodges, Pennsylvania among them, continue to call their Book of Constitutions, The Ahiman Rezon.

Anderson himself is still on the rack of criticism. Learned brethren are checking this, sifting through pages and leaving no stone unturned in order to appraise correctly his contributions to masonic history. But there is not so much disagreement on the Constitution. In that document, which did not give satisfaction to many upon its appearance, Anderson, as Brother Lionel Vibert has well said, "builded better than he knew," because he produced a document which until now serves as the groundwork of nearly all Grand Lodge Constitutions having jurisdiction over Symbolic Masonry, and which once and for all established Speculative Freemasonry on a basis apart, and with no sectarian character, either as to religion or politics. For all his faults as a historian (and these faults were as much of his age as of his own shortcomings), Anderson is a great figure in our annals and deserves at the hand of every student a careful and, reverent study.

IV. Conclusion

In concluding this very brief and inconclusive sketch of a great subject, I return to my first statement. In the whole circle of masonic studies there is not, for us Americans at any rate, any subject of such importance as this of the Old Charges, especially insofar as they have to do with our own Constitutions and Regulations, and that is very much indeed. Many false conceptions of Freemasonry may be directly traced to an unlearned, or wilful misinterpretation of the Old Charges, what they are, what they mean to us, and what their authority may be. In this land jurisprudence is a problem of supreme importance, and in a way not very well comprehended by our brethren in other parts, who often wonder why we should be so obsessed by it. We have forty-nine Grand Lodges, each of which is sovereign in its own state, and all of which must maintain fraternal relations with scores of Grand bodies abroad as well as with each other. These Grand Lodges assemble each year to legislate for the Craft, and therefore, in the very nature of things, the organization and government of the Order is for us Americans a much more complicated and important thing than it can be in other lands. To know what the Old Charges are, and to understand masonic constitutional law and practice, is for our leaders and law-givers a prime necessity.

Works Consulted in Preparing this Article

Gould's History of Freemasonry, Vol. 1, beginning on page 56; A.Q.C., I, 127; A.Q.C., I, 147; A.Q.C., I, 152; A.Q.C., IV, 73; A.Q.C., IV, 83; A.Q.C., IV, 171; A.Q.C., V, 37; A.Q.C., IV, 201; A.Q.C, IV, 36,198; A.Q.C., VII, 119; A.Q.C., VIII, 224; Hughan, *Old Charges*; A.Q.C., IX, 18; A.Q.C., IX, 85; A.Q.C., XI, 205; A.Q.C., XIV, 153; A.Q.C., XVI, 4; A.Q.C., XVIII, 16; A.Q.C., XX, 249; A.Q.C., XXI, 161, 211; A.Q.C., XXVIII, 189; *Gould's Concise History*, chapter V; Gould, *Collected Essays*, 3; Stillson, *History of Freemasonry and Concordant Orders*, 157; A.Q.C., XXXIII, 5; *The masonic Review*, Vol. XIII, 297; Edward Conder, *Records of the Hole Craft and Fellowship of Masons*; Vibert, *Story of the Craft*; Vibert, *Freemasonry Before the Era of Grand Lodge*; Findel, *History of Freemasonry*; Hughan, *Cole's Constitutions*; Fort, *Early History and Antiquities of Freemasonry*; Pierson, *Traditions, Origin and Early History of Freemasonry*; Hughan, *Ancient masonic Rolls*: Waite, *New Encyclopedia of Freemasonry*; Clegg, *Mackey's Revised History*; Ward, *Freemasonry and the Ancient Gods*: A.Q.C., Antigapha, all volumes.

The Old Charges and What They Mean to Us

Supplementary References: *Mackey's Encyclopedia* (Revised Edition). *Ahiman Rezon*, 37; *Antients*, 55; *Ars Quatuor Coronatorum*, 80; *Arts*, 80; Benjamin Cole, 157; *Charges of 1722*, 143; *Congregations*, 174; *Cooke's Manuscript*, 178; Dr. James Anderson, 57; Dr. Robert Plot, 570; *Four Crowned Martyrs*, 272; George B.F. Kloss, 383; *Gothic Constitutions*, 304; *Halliwell Manuscript*, 316; John Entick, 246; Laurence Dermott, 206; *Legend*, 433; *Legend of the Craft*, 434; *Old Charges*, 143; *Old Manuscripts*, 464; *Old Records*, 612; *Old Regulations*, 527; *Operative Masonry*, 532; *Parts*, 544; *Plot Manuscript*, 569; *Points*, 572; *Regius Manuscript*, 616; *Roberts' Manuscript*, 627; *Speculative Masonry*, 704.

Freemasonry And The Comacine Masters
by H. L. Haywood
The Builder - October 1923

In a chapter on the Roman Collegia published last June I referred briefly to the Comacine builder guilds as forming a bridge between the ancient classical culture of Rome and the medieval civilization which grew up after the barbarian invasions had ceased, leaving Europe in a state of more or less quiet. It is now in order to proceed farther into that subject, for it is one that will pay careful examination, especially since so much is being written about it these days pro and con. One friend and brother, who has a name among Masonic scholars, exclaimed in a recent letter, "I have grown weary of hearing about those blessed Comacines, and how Freemasonry sprang out of their loins, and how they kept the light burning in the Middle Ages. The truth is we know nothing about them." I could not agree with this colleague because he is undoubtedly wrong in saying that we know nothing about the Comacine masters - we know a great deal - but I could understand why he should be so impatient of those enthusiasts who have been claiming far more for the Comacines than the facts warrant. It will not be our purpose here to attempt to settle the problem one way or another; a setting forth of such facts as are known, with a brief sketch of the theory concerning their bearing on the history of Freemasonry, will satisfy our present needs.

The Comacine theory was first brought to the attention of the English-speaking Masonic world by a woman, Mrs. Lucy Baxter, who, writing over the penname of "Leader Scott", published in 1899 a remarkable volume entitled The Cathedral Builders; The Story of a Great Masonic Guild, with eighty-three illustrations, issued by Simpson Low, Marston and Company, London. The book is now unfortunately out of print, and growing more scarce all the while, with a rapidly mounting price. This work of 435 pages was followed in 1910 by a kind of codicil, in the shape of a small volume of eighty pages, by our faithful and beloved friend, Brother W. Ravenscroft, called The Comacines, Their Predecessors and Their Successors, afterwards published as a serial in THE BUILDER, along with many illustrations, and then reissued in book form. Except for scattered references in histories and encyclopedias these two books comprise the sole literary sources for English-spe aking Masons, but there is quite an abundant literature on the subject in Italian, some of which should be translated and published in America.

I. History of the Comacies

As we have already seen, the arts and crafts of the Roman Empire were rigidly organized into guilds, or collegia, each of which had in monopolistic control some one business, profession or handicraft. These were destroyed by the barbarians along with the towns and communities in which they were located, but a few of them, at Constantinople and in Rome particularly, survived the holocaust. It is believed that a collegium, or a few collegia, of architects and their workmen continued in the diocese of Como, situated in the Lombard kingdom of Northern Italy, on and about the lovely Lake Como, which included the districts of Mendrisio, Lugano, Bellinzona and Magadino. Why they remained there is a mystery, but it is believed that the presence of large stone quarries in that region was one reason, and that the strength and relatively high development of the Lombardic state was another. This region, many suppose, remained their seat and center for cent uries; hence, their name, "Comacini."

"The expression 'magistri Comacine'," writes Rivoira in his magnificent Lombardic Architecture (Vol. 1, p. 108), "appears for the first time in the code of the Lombard king, Rotharis (636-652), where, in the laws numbered CXLIII and CXLV, they figure as Master Masons with full and unlimited powers to make contracts and subcontracts for building works; to have their collegantes or 'colleagues' partners, members of the guild or fraternity, call them what you will - and lastly, their serfs (servi) or workmen a nd labourers." Rivoira says that in the region of Como guilds, or collegia, had never come to an end, and that many stone, marble and timber yards existed there to attract such workmen.

In his *History of Italian Architecture* Ricci states that the Comacine guilds were made free and independent of medieval restraints and set at liberty to travel about at will, but that statement has received no confirmation in Papal Bulls, the Acts of the Carolingian Kings, or in any of the authentic annalists, though search has often been made, and was made at Rome long before there existed any prejudice against Freemasonry in that quarter. The Comacines extended their influence and activities in the same way as other guilds, by invitation and contract, and by organization of lodges in new towns.

When St. Boniface went to Germany as a missionary, Pope Gregory II gave "him credentials, instructions, etc., and sent with him a large following of monks, versed in the art of building, and of lay brethren who were also architects, to assist them." Italian chroniclers say that when the monk Augustine was sent in A.D. 598 as a missionary to convert the British, Pope Gregory sent along several Masons with him, and that Augustine later on sent back for more men capable of building churches, oratories and mona steries. Leader Scott believes that in both these instances the workmen sent were Comacine masters and bases her contention on the evidence of building methods and styles employed. Similarly, she traces the Comacines into Sicily, Normandy, and into all the large centers of Southern, Italy, in this way explaining how, by a gradual circling outward, the Comacine fraternity of builders came at last to work in nearly all parts of Europe and Britain.

On page 159 of her book Leader Scott gives a valuable summary of the history of the Comacines, basing it largely, one may suppose, on Merzario's I Maestri Comacini, Vol I, a treatise that should by all means be translated and published in this country.

"Let us restate the argument briefly-

1. When Italy was overrun by the barbarians, Roman Collegia were everywhere suppressed.

2. The architectural college of Rome is said to have removed from that city to the republic of Comum.

3. In early medieval times, one of the most important Masonic guilds in Europe was the Society of Comacine masters, which in its constitution, methods and work was essentially Roman, and seems to have been the survival of this Roman college.

4. Italian chroniclists assert that architects and masons accompanied Augustine to land, and later Italian continental writers of repute adopted that view.

5. Whether this is proved or not, it was customary for missionaries to take in their train persons experienced in building,

and if Augustine did not do go, his practice was an exception to what seems to have been a general rule. Besides, a band of forty monks would have been useless to him unless some of them could follow a secular calling useful to the mission, for they were unacquainted with the British language and could not act independently.

6. Masonic monks were not uncommon, and there were such monks associated with the Comacine body; so that qualified architects were easily found in the ranks of the religious orders.

7. From Bede's account of the settlement of Augustine's mission in Britain, it seems clear that he must have brought Masonic architects with him.

8. Gregory would be likely to choose architects for the mission from the Comacine Order, which held the old Roman traditions of building, rather than those of a Byzantine guild, and the record of their work in Britain proves that he did.

9. In Saxon as in the earlier Comacine carvings there are frequent representations of fabulous monsters, symbolical birds and beasts, the subjects of some of these carvings being suggested, apparently, by the Physiologists, which had a Latin origin.

10. In the writings of the Venerable Bede and Richard, Prior of Hagustald, we meet with phrases and words which are in the Edict of King Rotharis of 643, and in the Memoratorio of 713 of King Luitprand, which show that these writers were familiar with certain terms of art used by the Comacine masters.

If this account be true it is of inestimable importance to us as giving an explanation of how the arts of civilization, long supposed to have become extinct during the Dark Ages, were never extinct at all but were continued in preservation by the workmen and artists in the Comacine guilds. Those men were more than builders, for they were skilled in many other crafts beside, and understood sculpture, painting, Cosmati work or mosaic, wood work and carving, and also, it may well be, literature and music, alo ng with many other accomplishments belonging; to the civil arts. Like one ship crossing a stormy sea into which all its sister vessels had sunk, the organization of the Comacine masters preserved the ark of civilization until such time as the hurricane cleared from Europe and the seething barbarian tribes themselves became ready for peace and communal life. If there is any unbroken continuity in the history of architecture, if builder guilds of a more modern period can trace any of their arts, traditions a nd customs back to ancient times, it is through the Comacines that the chain was kept unbroken in the Dark Ages.

It must not be supposed that all this has as yet been solidly established; the Comacine Theory continues to be a theory. Rivoira, who is always so careful, is cautious against accepting too much. He says that we know little about their manner of organization, or about the terms connected with them, schola, loggia, etc. But even so he attributes to them great histories importance, not only as serving as a link with the ancient collegia, but also as paving the way for the magnificent renaissance of art and civilization which as seen in our first chapter in this series, burst into flower in Gothic architecture. His following words bear witness to that.

> "Whatever may have been the organization of the Comacine or Lombard guilds, and however these may have been affected by outward events, they did not cease to exist in consequence by of the fall of the Lombard kingdom. With the first breath of municipal freedom, and with the rise of the new brotherhoods of artisans, they, too, perhaps, may have reformed themselves like the latter who were nothing but the continuation of the 'collegium' of Roman times preserving its existence through the barbarian ages, and transformed little by little into the medieval corporation. The members may have found themselves constrained to enter into a more perfect unity of thought and sentiment, to bind themselves into a more compact body, and thus put themselves in a condition to maintain their ancient supremacy in carrying out the most important building works in Italy. But we cannot say anything more. And even putting aside all tradition, the monuments themselves are t here to confirm what we have said."

Merzario, not quite as cautious as Rivoira, bears witness in the same manner:

"In this darkness which extended over all Italy, only one small lamp remained alight, making a bright spark in the vast Italian necropolis. It was from the Magistri Comacini. Their respective names are unknown, their individual works unspecialized, but the breath of their spirit might be felt all through those centuries, and their name collectively is legion. We may safely say that of all the works of art between A.D. 800 and 1000, the greater and better part are due to that brotherhood - always faithful and often secret - of the Magistri Comacini. The authority and judgment of learned men justify the assertion."

Signor Agostino Segredio is similarly convinced, and so expresses himself in a passage quoted on page 56 of Ravenscroft's The Comacines:

"While we are speaking of the Masonic Companies and their jealous secrecy we must not forget the most grand and potent guild of the Middle Ages, that of the Freemasons; originating most probably from the builders of Como (Magistri Comacini). it spread beyond the Alps. Popes gave them their benediction, monarchs protected them, and the most powerful thought it an honour to be inscribed in their ranks. They with the utmost jealousy practised all the arts connected with building, and by severe laws and penalties (perhaps also with bloodshed) prohibited others from the practice of building important edifices. Long and hard were the initiations to aspirants, and mysterious were the meetings and the teaching, and to enable themselves they dated their origin from Solomon's Temple."

And so also Leader Scott, who Sums up the matter in a sentence:

"Thus, though there is no certain proof that the Comacines were the veritable stock from which the pseudo-Freemasonry of the present day sprang, we may at least admit that they were a link between the classis Collegia and all other art and trade guilds of the Middle Ages."

Brother Joseph Fort Newton accepts this interpretation in The Builder's, where, on page 86, he writes:

> "With the breaking up of the College of Architects and their expulsion from Rome, we come upon a period in which it is hard to follow their path. Happily the task has been made less baffling by recent research, and if we are unable to trace them all the way much light has been let into the darkness. Hitherto there has been a hiatus also in the history of architecture between the classic art of Rome, which is said to have died when the empire fell to pieces, and the rise of Gothic art. Just so, in the story the builders one finds a gap of like length, between the Collegia of Rome and the cathedral artists. While the gap cannot, as yet be perfectly bridged, much has been done to that end by Leader Scott in The Cathedral Builders; The Story of a Great Masonic Guild - a book itself a work of art as well as of fine scholarship. Her thesis is that the missing link is to be found in the Magistri Comacini, a guild of architects who, on the break-up of the Roman Empire, fled to Comacina, a fortified island in Lake Como, and there kept alive the traditions of classic art during the Dark Ages; that from them were developed in direct descent the various styles of Italian architecture; and that, finally, they carried the knowledge and practice of architecture and sculpture into France, Spain, Germany and England. Such a thesis is difficult, and from its nature not susceptible of absolute proof, but the writer makes it as certain as anything can well be."

On the other side are authorities who deny the existence of any such fraternity as the Comacines, or else give them a minor place in the history of medieval architecture. R.F. Gould, in the original edition of his Conche History, page 105, speaks his mind clearly:

> "At the present day the idea of there having been, in the early part of the thirteenth century, Colleges of Masons in every country of Europe, which received the blessing of the

Holy See, under an injunction of dedicating their skill to the erection of ecclesiastical buildings, may be dismissed chimerical. Though I must not forget that, according to the well-known and highly imaginative Historical Essay on Architecture (1835) of Mr. Hope - who greatly expands the meaning of two passages in the works of Muratori - a body of traveling architects, who wandered over Europe during the Middle Ages, received the appellation of Magistri Comacini, or Masters of Como, a title which became generic to all those of the profession. The idea has been revived by a recent writer, who believes that these Magistri Comacini were a survival of the Roman Collegia, that they settled in Como and were afterwards employed by the Lombard kings, under whose patronage they developed a powerful and highly organized guild, with a dominant influence on the whole architecture of the Middle Ages (The Cathedral Builders). But, even if such a theory had any probability, it would be far from clearing up certain obscurities in the history of medieval architecture, as the author suggests would be the case. Interchanges of influence were not uncommon, but the works of local schools present far too marked an individuality to render it possible that they could owe much (if anything) to the influence of any central guild."

On page 175 of the same work Gould refers to George Edmund Street as saying that such a theory as that of the Comacines "seems to me to be altogether erroneous"; Wyatt Papworth as saying that "I believe they never existed"; and on the preceding pages prints a long excerpt from Dr. Milman to the same effect.

It appears to me that this opposition is a reaction to an exaggeration of the Comacine argument. Leader Scott does not claim for them that they themselves laid out European civilization, or founded Gothic architecture (as Dr. Newton appears to do, and which is most certainly an error), or that the founding of all the medieval architectural styles was their work; she holds merely that in and around Lake Como there long existed a guild of architects, and to this guild traced many influences; their influence in various lands she suggests by way of cautious tentative theories, and never wearies of warning her reader that she is feeling her way through the dark; and she believes that the history of this Comacine guild may be traced back to very ancient days, and may be very probably linked on to the history of the Roman collegia.

II. The Comacines and Freemasonry

We Masons have long ceased to be moved by the vulgar desire to claim for our Fraternity an impossible antiquity, as if it had been organized by Adam in the Garden of Eden, or was, as one old worthy expressed it, diffused through space before God created the world. Freemasonry is old enough as it is, and honourable enough, not to require that we embellish it by a fabulous lineage. We know that it came into existence gradually, like everything else in our human world, here a little and there a little, and that it was no more miraculous in the past than it is now. At the same time we are interested to observe the rise and prosperity of organizations similar to it, or prophetic of it, wherever or whenever they may have come into existence. The use of cooperation and of fraternity, the employment of the device of secrecy and loyalty to aims above the present moment, the contemplation of such endeavors by our striving fellow men, toiling in the dim twilights of life, is always an inspiration, and helps to set a glow the ideals of our own Masonry hidden away in the recesses of our souls. It is from such a point of view, I believe, that we should look upon the story of the Comacines; I have not been able to persuade myself that they were in any accurate use of the word Freemasons, or that our own Fraternity has had any but the most tenuous and general historic connections with the lodges of those old masters. The story of our Craft is intertwined with the history of architecture, so that any new light on the latte r helps us the better to understand the evolution of the former; in this sense, and in the sense defined just above, the story of the Comacines is of value to us, but not as comprising a chapter in the known veridical history of Masonry. The Comacine guild was in many respects similar to the Masonic guilds that came after, and which served as the roots from which Symbolical Masonry ultimately developed, but to see in the Comacine guild the immediate parent of the Masonic guild is not possible, it seems to me, unless we are to trust too much to imagination or are willing to stretch the word "Freemasonry" to mean more than it should. My own theory, which will be elaborated step by step as these chapters proceed, is that Freemasonry strictly so-called originated in England and in England only that it had its gradual rise among the guilds that grew up with Gothic architecture; that a germ of moralism, religion and ceremonialism in those guilds, chancing to find itself in a favoring environment, outgrew the operative element until in the seventeenth century lodges began to become wholly speculative; that in this time of transition new elements were introduced from certain occult sources; and that this evolution culminated at last in 1717 with the founding of the Mother Grand Lodge at London, from which all modern Freemasonry has been subsequently derived. I have not been able to satisfy myself, though I have had the will to try, that our Masonry was given to us by the Comacine masters.

Leader Scott herself, whose knowledge of Freemasonry was even less than her opinion of it, was very careful not to confuse the Freemasonry of today with what she rather loosely (too loosely, one may think) calls the "Freemasonry" of the Comacine guild. The passage in which she expresses herself is almost always quoted only in part; I shall give it in full, not only as showing her own theory of the historical connections between the two, but also as revealing her unfortunate lack of knowledge of Masonry as i t exists today. The passage quoted begins on page 16 of her book:

> "Since I began writing this chapter a curious chance has brought into my hands an old Italian book on the institutions, rites and ceremonies of the Order of Freemasons. Of course the anonymous writer begins with Adoniram, the architect of Solomon's Temple, who had so very many workmen to pay that, not being able to distinguish them by name, he divided them into three different classes, novices, operatori and magistri, and to; each class gave a secret set of signs and passwords, so that from these their fee s could be easily fixed and imposture avoided. It is interesting to know that precisely the same divisions and classes existed in the Roman Collegium and

the Comacine Guild - and that, as in Solomon's time, the great symbols of the order were the endless knot or Solomon's knot, and the 'Lion of Judah.'

"Our author goes on to tell of the second revival of Freemasonry, in its present entirely spiritual significance, and he gives Oliver Cromwell, of all people, the credit of this revival! The rites and ceremonies he describes are the greatest tissue of medieval superstition, child's play, blood-curdling oaths and mysterious secrecy with nothing to conceal that can be imagined. All the signs of Masonry without a figment of reality; every moral thing masquerades under an architectural aspect, and that 'Temple made without hands' which is figured by a Freemason's lodge in these days. But the significant point is that all these names and Masonic emblems point to something real which existed at some long-past time, and, as far as regards the organization and nomenclature, we find the whole thing in its vital and actual working form in the Comacine guild. Our nameless Italian who reveals all the Masonic secrets, tells us that every lodge has three divisions, one for the novices, one for the operatori or working brethren, and one for the masters. Now wherever we find the Comacines at work we find the threefold organization of schola or school for the novices, laborerium for the operatori, and the Opera or Fabbrica for the Masters of Administration.

"The anonymous one tells us that there is a Gran Maestro or Arch-magister at the head of the whole order, a Capo Maestro or chief master at the head of each lodge. Every lodge must besides be provided with two or four Soprastanti, a treasurer and a secretary-general, besides accountants. This is precisely what we find in the organization of the Comacine lodges. As we follow them through the centuries we shall see it appearing in city after city, at first fully revealed by the books of the treasurers and Soprastanti themselves, in Siena, Florence and Milan.

"Thus, though there is no certain proof that the Comacines were the veritable stock from which the pseudo-Masonry of the present day sprang, we may at least admit that they were a link between the classic Collegia and all other art and trade Guilds of the Middle Ages."

The analogies between the two briefly referred to in this quoted passage, might be expanded. The Comacines had lodges, Grand Masters, secrets (they kept a secret book called L'Arcano Magistero), wore aprons, kept a chest, dispensed charity, possessed means of identification, and employed much symbolism of which some items are familiar to us, as King Solomon's knot the Lion of Judah, the two Great Pillars "J" and "B"; square, compasses, mosaic pavement, etc. Also there was a certain gradation among them, similar to our degrees, though I have failed to discover any evidence of an initiation.

Brother Ravenscroft, with whom one is loathe ever to disagree and who continues his researches in this field, may be right in thinking that some ancient Masonic traditions, particularly such as had to do with Solomon's Temple, were preserved and transmitted to us out of antiquity by the Comacines. It is a fascinating theory to which future discoveries may bring more convincing proof; it would seem to me, if I may again express a private opinion, that two facts tell heavily against such a theory; one is that these traditions, most of them at least, have always been preserved in the Scriptures and therefore available at any time; and, what is more important, there was no known connection between the Comacine guild, which did its own work in Italy where Gothic never became established, and the guilds among which Gothic grew up.

The whole Comacine question, so far as speculative Freemasonry is concerned, it thus appears, remains in the air, or, if one prefers the figure, on the knees of the gods. This means that there is much work remaining to be done by students of today, who will find themselves, if they will turn their attention to medieval architecture and its history, in an enchanted realm.

Edict of Rothari
(The Comacine Masters)
A.D. 643

INCIPIT EDICTVM QVEM RENOVAVIT DOMINVS ROTHARI

144. De magistros commacinos. Si magister commacinus cum collegantes suos cuiuscumque domum ad restaurandam vel fabricandam super se, placitum finito de mercedes, susceperit et contigerit aliquem per ipsam domum aut materium elapsum aut lapidem mori, non requiratur a domino, cuius domus fuerit, nisi magister commacinus cum consortibus suis ipsum homicidium aut damnum conponat; quia, postquam fabulam firmam de mercedis pro suo lucro suscepit, non inmerito damnum sustinet.

145. De rogatos aut conductos magistros. Si quis magistrum commacinum unum aut plures rogaverit aut conduxerit ad opera dictandum aut solatium diurnum prestandum inter servûs suos, domum aut casa sibi facienda, et contegerit per ipsam casam aliquem ex ipsis commacinis mori, non requiratur ab ipso, cuius casa est. Nam si cadens arbor aut lapis ex ipsa fabrigam occiderit aliquem extraneum, aut quodlebit damnum fecerit, non repotetur culpa magistris, sed ille, qui conduxit, ipse damnum susteneat.

English Translation

Section 144. Of the Comacine Master - If a Comacine Master with his associates (colligantes) shall undertake to restore or build the house of any person whatsoever, after an agreement shall have been closed as to payment, and it chances that someone should be killed, by reason of the house, through the falling of either material or stone, no claim shall be lodged against the owner of the house, in case the Comacine Master or those working with him (consortibus) shall fall to settle for the death or the damage done; because who after having contracted to do work f or his own advantage, must assume, not undeservedly, the damage done.

Edict of Rothari

Section 145. Of masters called or brought in. - If any person shall call or bring in Comacine Masters one or several - to design a work or to daily assist his retainers (servi) at the building of his house (domun aut casa), and it should happen that, by reason of this house (casa), one of the Comacines is killed, the owner of the house (casa) shall not be held responsible. On the other hand, if falling timber or stone should kill an outsider or cause injury to anyone, the fault shall not be imputed to the Masters, but to him who called them in, and he shall be responsible for the damage.

Translated by Ossian Lang, Grand Historian,
The Grand Lodge of New York, 1925

Regius Manuscript
(The Halliwell Manuscript)
A Poem of Moral Duties
circa 1390
Original and Modern Text

(Modern Text)

Here begin the constitutions of the art of Geometry according to Euclid.

Whoever will both well read and look
He may find written in old book
Of great lords and also ladies,
That had many children together, y-wisse; (certainly)
And had no income to keep them with,
Neither in town nor field nor frith (enclosed wood);
A council together they could them take,
To ordain for these children's sake,
How they might best lead their life
Without great dis-ease, care, and strife;
And most for the multitude that was coming
Of their children after their ending
They send them after great clerks,
To teach them then good works;

And pray we them, for our Lord's sake.
To our children some work to make,
That they might get their living thereby,
Both well and honestly full securely.
In that time, through good geometry,
This honest craft of good masonry
Was ordained and made in this manner,
Counterfeited of these clerks together;
At these lord's prayers they counterfeited geometry,
And gave it the name of masonry,
For the most honest craft of all.

These lords' children thereto did fall,
To learn of him the craft of geometry,
The which he made full curiously;
Through fathers' prayers and mothers' also,
This honest craft he put them to.
He learned best, and was of honesty,
And passed his fellows in curiosity,
If in that craft he did him pass,
He should have more worship than the lasse, (less)
This great clerk's name was Euclid,
His name it spread full wonder wide.
Yet this great clerk ordained he
To him that was higher in this degree,
That he should teach the simplest of wit
In that honest craft to be parfytte; (perfect)
And so each one shall teach the other,
And love together as sister and brother.

Furthermore yet that ordained he,
Master called so should he be;
So that he were most worshipped,
Then should he be so called;
But masons should never one another call,
Within the craft amongst them all,
Neither subject nor servant, my dear brother,
Though he be not so perfect as is another;
Each shall call other fellows by cuthe, (friendship)
Because they come of ladies' birth.
On this manner, through good wit of geometry,
Began first the craft of masonry;
The clerk Euclid on this wise it found,
This craft of geometry in Egypt land.

In Egypt he taught it full wide,
In divers lands on every side;
Many years afterwards, I understand,
Ere that the craft came into this land.
This craft came into England, as I you say,

Regius Manuscript (Modern Text)

In time of good King Athelstane's day;
He made then both hall and even bower,
And high temples of great honour,
To disport him in both day and night,
And to worship his God with all his might.
This good lord loved this craft full well,
And purposed to strengthen it every del, (part)
For divers faults that in the craft he found;
He sent about into the land

After all the masons of the craft,
To come to him full even straghfte, (straight)
For to amend these defaults all
By good counsel, if it might fall.
An assembly then he could let make
Of divers lords in their state,
Dukes, earls, and barons also,
Knights, squires and many mo, (more)
And the great burgesses of that city,
They were there all in their degree;
There were there each one algate, (always)
To ordain for these masons' estate,
There they sought by their wit,
How they might govern it;

Fifteen articles they there sought,
And fifteen points there they wrought,

Here begins the first article.

The first article of this geometry;-
The master mason must be full securely
Both steadfast, trusty and true,
It shall him never then rue;
And pay thy fellows after the cost,
As victuals goeth then, well thou woste; (knowest)
And pay them truly, upon thy fay, (faith)
What they deserven may; (may deserve)

And to their hire take no more,
But what that they may serve for;
And spare neither for love nor drede, (dread)

Of neither parties to take no mede; (bribe)
Of lord nor fellow, whoever he be,
Of them thou take no manner of fee;
And as a judge stand upright,
And then thou dost to both good right;
And truly do this wheresoever thou gost, (goest)
Thy worship, thy profit, it shall be most.

Second article.

The second article of good masonry,
As you must it here hear specially,
That every master, that is a mason,
Must be at the general congregation,
So that he it reasonably be told
Where that the assembly shall be holde; (held)

And to that assembly he must needs gon, (go)
Unless he have a reasonable skwasacyon, (excuse)
Or unless he be disobedient to that craft
Or with falsehood is over-raft, (overtaken)
Or else sickness hath him so strong,
That he may not come them among;
That is an excuse good and able,
To that assembly without fable.

Third article.

The third article forsooth it is,
That the master takes to no 'prentice,
Unless he have good assurance to dwell
Seven years with him, as I you tell,
His craft to learn, that is profitable;

Regius Manuscript (Modern Text)

Within less he may not be able
To lords' profit, nor to his own
As you may know by good reason.

Fourth article.

The fourth article this must be,
That the master him well besee,
That he no bondman 'prentice make,
Nor for no covetousness do him take;
For the lord that he is bound to,
May fetch the 'prentice wheresoever he go.
If in the lodge he were ty-take, (taken)
Much dis-ease it might there make,
And such case it might befal,
That it might grieve some or all.

For all the masons that be there
Will stand together all y-fere. (together)
If such one in that craft should dwell,
Of divers dis-eases you might tell;
For more ease then, and of honesty,
Take a 'prentice of higher degree.
By old time written I find
That the 'prentice should be of gentle kind;
And so sometime, great lords' blood
Took this geometry that is full good.

Fifth article.

The fifth article is very good,
So that the 'prentice be of lawful blood;
The master shall not, for no advantage,

Make no 'prentice that is outrage; (deformed)
It is to mean, as you may hear
That he have all his limbs whole all y-fere; (together)
To the craft it were great shame,

To make a halt man and a lame,
For an imperfect man of such blood
Should do the craft but little good.
Thus you may know every one,
The craft would have a mighty man;
A maimed man he hath no might,
You must it know long ere night.

Sixth article.

The sixth article you must not miss

That the master do the lord no prejudice,
To take the lord for his 'prentice,
As much as his fellows do, in all wise.
For in that craft they be full perfect,
So is not he, you must see it.
Also it were against good reason,
To take his hire as his fellows don. (do)
This same article in this case,
Judgeth his prentice to take less
Than his fellows, that be full perfect.
In divers matters, know requite it,
The master may his 'prentice so inform,
That his hire may increase full soon,

And ere his term come to an end,
His hire may full well amend.

Seventh article.

The seventh article that is now here,
Full well will tell you all y-fere (together)
That no master for favour nor dread,
Shall no thief neither clothe nor feed.
Thieves he shall harbour never one,
Nor him that hath killed a man,
Nor the same that hath a feeble name,

Lest it would turn the craft to shame.

Eighth article.

The eighth article sheweth you so,
That the master may it well do.
If that he have any man of craft,
And he be not so perfect as he ought,
He may him change soon anon,
And take for him a more perfect man.
Such a man through rechalaschepe, (recklessness)
Might do the craft scant worship.

Ninth article.

The ninth article sheweth full well,
That the master be both wise and felle; (strong)
That he no work undertake,
Unless he can both it end and make;
And that it be to the lords' profit also,

And to his craft, wheresoever he go;
And that the ground be well y-take, (taken)
That it neither flaw nor grake. (crack)

Tenth article.

The tenth article is for to know,
Among the craft, to high and low,
There shall no master supplant another,
But be together as sister and brother,
In this curious craft, all and some,
That belongeth to a master mason.
Nor shall he supplant no other man,
That hath taken a work him upon,
In pain thereof that is so strong,

That weigheth no less than ten ponge, (pounds)

but if that he be guilty found,
That took first the work on hand;
For no man in masonry
Shall not supplant other securely,
But if that it be so wrought,
That in turn the work to nought;
Then may a mason that work crave,
To the lords' profit for it to save
In such a case if it do fall,
There shall no mason meddle withal.
Forsooth he that beginneth the ground,
If he be a mason good and sound,
He hath it securely in his mind

To bring the work to full good end.

Eleventh article.

The eleventh article I tell thee,
That he is both fair and free;
For he teacheth, by his might,
That no mason should work by night,
But if be in practising of wit,
If that I could amend it.

Twelfth article.

The twelfth article is of high honesty
To every mason wheresoever he be,
He shall not his fellows' work deprave,
If that he will his honesty save;
With honest words he it commend,

By the wit God did thee send;
But it amend by all that thou may,
Between you both without nay. (doubt)

Regius Manuscript (Modern Text)

Thirteenth article.

The thirteenth article, so God me save,
Is if that the master a 'prentice have,
Entirely then that he him teach,
And measurable points that he him reche, (tell)
That he the craft ably may conne, (know)
Wheresoever he go under the sun.

Fourteenth article.

The fourteenth article by good reason,
Sheweth the master how he shall don; (do)
He shall no 'prentice to him take,

Unless diver cares he have to make,
That he may within his term,
Of him divers points may learn.

Fifteenth article.

The fifteenth article maketh an end,
For to the master he is a friend;
To teach him so, that for no man,
No false maintenance he take him upon,
Nor maintain his fellows in their sin,
For no good that he might win;
Nor no false oath suffer him to make,
For dread of their souls' sake,
Lest it would turn the craft to shame,
And himself to very much blame.

Plural constitutions.

At this assembly were points ordained mo, (more)
Of great lords and masters also.
That who will know this craft and come to estate,
He must love well God and holy church algate, (always)

And his master also that he is with,
Wheresoever he go in field or frythe, (enclosed wood)
And thy fellows thou love also,
For that thy craft will that thou do.

Second Point.

The second point as I you say,
That the mason work upon the work day,
As truly as he can or may,
To deserve his hire for the holy-day,
And truly to labour on his deed,
Well deserve to have his mede. (reward)

Third point.

The third point must be severele, (severely)
With the 'prentice know it well,
His master's counsel he keep and close,
And his fellows by his good purpose;
The privities of the chamber tell he no man,
Nor in the lodge whatsoever they don; (do)
Whatsoever thou hearest or seest them do,
Tell it no man wheresoever you go;
The counsel of hall, and even of bower,

Keep it well to great honour,
Lest it would turn thyself to blame,
And bring the craft into great shame.

Fourth point.

The fourth point teacheth us alse, (also)
That no man to his craft be false;
Error he shall maintain none
Against the craft, but let it gone; (go)
Nor no prejudice he shall not do
To his master, nor his fellow also;

Regius Manuscript (Modern Text)

And though the 'prentice be under awe,
Yet he would have the same law.

Fifth point.

The fifth point is without nay, (doubt)
That when the mason taketh his pay
Of the master, ordained to him,
Full meekly taken so must it byn; (be)
Yet must the master by good reason,
Warn him lawfully before noon,
If he will not occupy him no more,
As he hath done there before;
Against this order he may not strive,
If he think well for to thrive.

Sixth point.

The sixth point is full given to know,
Both to high and even to low,

For such case it might befall;
Among the masons some or all,
Through envy or deadly hate,
Oft ariseth full great debate.
Then ought the mason if that he may,
Put them both under a day;
But loveday yet shall they make none,
Till that the work-day be clean gone
Upon the holy-day you must well take
Leisure enough loveday to make,
Lest that it would the work-day
Hinder their work for such a fray;
To such end then that you them draw.

That they stand well in God's law.

Seventh point.

The seventh point he may well mean,
Of well long life that God us lene, (lend)
As it descrieth well openly,
Thou shalt not by thy master's wife lie,
Nor by thy fellows', in no manner wise,
Lest the craft would thee despise;
Nor by thy fellows' concubine,
No more thou wouldst he did by thine.
The pain thereof let it be sure,
That he be 'prentice full seven year,
If he forfeit in any of them
So chastised then must he ben; (be)
Full much care might there begin,
For such a foul deadly sin.

Eighth point.

The eighth point, he may be sure,
If thou hast taken any cure,
Under thy master thou be true,
For that point thou shalt never rue;
A true mediator thou must needs be
To thy master, and thy fellows free;
Do truly all that thou might,
To both parties, and that is good right.

Ninth point.

The ninth point we shall him call,
That he be steward of our hall,
If that you be in chamber y-fere, (together)
Each one serve other with mild cheer;
Gentle fellows, you must it know,
For to be stewards all o-rowe, (in turn)
Week after week without doubt,
Stewards to be so all in turn about,

Amiably to serve each one other,
As though they were sister and brother;
There shall never one another costage (cost)
Free himself to no advantage,
But every man shall be equally free

In that cost, so must it be;
Look that thou pay well every man algate, (always)
That thou hast bought any victuals ate, (eaten)
That no craving be made to thee,
Nor to thy fellows in no degree,
To man or to woman, whoever he be,
Pay them well and truly, for that will we;
Thereof on thy fellow true record thou take,
For that good pay as thou dost make,
Lest it would thy fellow shame,
And bring thyself into great blame.
Yet good accounts he must make
Of such goods as he hath y-take (taken)
Of thy fellows' goods that thou hast spende, (spent)
Where and how and to what end;
Such accounts thou must come to,
When thy fellows wish that thou do.

Tenth point.

The tenth point presenteth well good life,
To live without care and strife;
For if the mason live amiss,
And in his work be false y-wisse, (I know)
And through such a false skewsasyon (excuse)
May slander his fellows without reason,
Through false slander of such fame.

May make the craft acquire blame.
If he do the craft such villainy,
Do him no favour then securely,
Nor maintain not him in wicked life,

Lest it would turn to care and strife;
But yet him you shall not delayme, (delay)
Unless that you shall him constrain,
For to appear wheresoever you will,
Where that you will, loud, or still;
To the next assembly you shall him call,
To appear before his fellows all,
And unless he will before them appear,

The craft he must need forswear;
He shall then be punished after the law
That was founded by old dawe. (day)

Eleventh point.

The eleventh point is of good discretion,
As you must know by good reason;
A mason, if he this craft well con, (know,
That seeth his fellow hew on a stone,
And is in point to spoil that stone,
Amend it soon if that thou can,
And teach him then it to amend,
That the lords' work be not y-schende, (spoiled)
And teach him easily it to amend,

With fair words, that God thee hath lende; (lent)
For his sake that sit above,
With sweet words nourish his love.

Twelfth point.

The twelfth point is of great royalty,
There as the assembly held shall be,
There shall be masters and fellows also,
And other great lords many mo; (more)
There shall be the sheriff of that country,
And also the mayor of that city,
Knights and squires there shall be,

Regius Manuscript (Modern Text)

And also aldermen, as you shall see;
Such ordinance as they make there,

They shall maintain it all y-fere (together)
Against that man, whatsoever he be,
That belongeth to the craft both fair and free.
If he any strife against them make,
Into their custody he shall be take. (taken)

Thirteenth point.

The thirteenth point is to us full lief,
He shall swear never to be no thief,
Nor succour him in his false craft,
For no good that he hath byraft; (bereft)
And thou must it know or sin,
Neither for his good, nor for his kin.

Fourteenth point.

The fourteenth point is full good law
To him that would be under awe;
A good true oath he must there swear
To his master and his fellows that be there;
He must be steadfast and also true
To all this ordinance, wheresoever he go,
And to his liege lord the king,
To be true to him over all thing.
And all these points here before

To them thou must need be y-swore, (sworn)
And all shall swear the same oath
Of the masons, be they lief be they loath.
To all these points here before,

That hath been ordained by full good lore.
And they shall enquire every man
Of his party, as well as he can,

If any man may be found guilty
In any of these points specially;
And who he be, let him be sought,
And to the assembly let him be brought.

Fifteen point.

The fifteenth point is of full good lore,
For them that shall be there y-swore, (sworn)
Such ordinance at the assembly was laid
Of great lords and masters before said;
For the same that be disobedient, y-wisse, (I know)

Against the ordinance that there is,
Of these articles that were moved there,
Of great lords and masons all y-fere, (together)
And if they be proved openly
Before that assembly, by and by,
And for their guilt's no amends will make,
Then must they need the craft forsake;
And no masons craft they shall refuse,
And swear it never more to use.
But if that they will amends make,
Again to the craft they shall never take;
And if that they will not do so,
The sheriff shall come them soon to,

And put their bodies in deep prison,
For the trespass that they have done,
And take their goods and their cattle
Into the king's hand, every delle, (part)
And let them dwell there full still,
Till it be our liege king's will.

Another ordinance of the art of geometry.

They ordained there an assembly to be y-holde, (hold)
Every year, wheresoever they would,

Regius Manuscript (Modern Text)

To amend the defaults, if any were found
Among the craft within the land;
Each year or third year it should be holde, (held)

In every place weresoever they would;
Time and place must be ordained also,
In what place they should assemble to,
All the men of craft there they must be,
And other great lords, as you must see,
To mend the faults that he there spoken,
If that any of them be then broken.
There they shall be all y-swore, (sworn)
That belongeth to this craft's lore,
To keep their statutes every one
That were ordained by King Athelstane;
These statutes that I have here found

I ordain they be held through my land,
For the worship of my royalty,
That I have by my dignity.
Also at every assembly that you hold,
That you come to your liege king bold,
Beseeching him of his high grace,
To stand with you in every place,
To confirm the statutes of King Athelstane,
That he ordained to this craft by good reason.

The art of the four crowned ones.

Pray we now to God almight, (almighty)
And to his mother Mary bright,

That we may keep these articles here,
And these points well all y-fere, (together)
As did these holy martyrs four,
That in this craft were of great honour;
They were as good masons as on earth shall go,
Gravers and image-makers they were also.

For they were workmen of the best,
The emperor had to them great luste; (liking)
He willed of them an image to make
That might be worshipped for his sake;
Such monuments he had in his dawe, (day)
To turn the people from Christ's law.

But they were steadfast in Christ's lay, (law)
And to their craft without nay; (doubt)
They loved well God and all his lore,
And were in his service ever more.
True men they were in that dawe, (day)
And lived well in God's law;
They thought no monuments for to make,
For no good that they might take,
To believe on that monument for their God,
They would not do so, though he were wod; (furious)
For they would not forsake their true fay, (faith)
And believe on his false lay, (law)
The emperor let take them soon anon,
And put them in a deep prison;
The more sorely he punished them in that place,
The more joy was to them of Christ's grace,
Then when he saw no other one,
To death he let them then gon; (go)
Whose will of their life yet more know
By the book he might it show
In the legend of sanctorum (holy ones)
The names of the quatuor coronatorum.
Their feast will be without nay, (doubt)
After Hallow-e'en the eighth day.
You may hear as I do read,
That many years after, for great dread
That Noah's flood was all run,
The tower of Babylon was begun,
As plain work of lime and stone,
As any man should look upon;
So long and broad it was begun,

Regius Manuscript (Modern Text)

Seven miles the height shadoweth the sun.
King Nebuchadnezzar let it make
To great strength for man's sake,

Though such a flood again should come,
Over the work it should not nome; (take)
For they had so high pride, with strong boast
All that work therefore was lost;
An angel smote them so with divers speech,
That never one knew what the other should tell.
Many years after, the good clerk Euclid
Taught the craft of geometry full wonder wide,
So he did that other time also,
Of divers crafts many mo. (more)
Through high grace of Christ in heaven,
He commenced in the sciences seven;

Grammar is the first science I know,
Dialect the second, so I have I bliss,
Rhetoric the third without nay, (doubt)
Music is the fourth, as I you say,
Astronomy is the fifth, by my snout,
Arithmetic the sixth, without doubt,
Geometry the seventh maketh an end,
For he is both meek and hende, (courteous)
Grammar forsooth is the root,
Whoever will learn on the book;
But art passeth in his degree,
As the fruit doth the root of the tree;

Rhetoric measureth with ornate speech among,
And music it is a sweet song;
Astronomy numbereth, my dear brother,
Arithmetic sheweth one thing that is another,
Geometry the seventh science it is,
That can separate falsehood from truth, I know.
These be the sciences seven,
Who useth them well he may have heaven.

Ancient Manuscripts of the Freemasons

Now dear children by your wit
Pride and covetousness that you leave it,
And taketh heed to good discretion,
And to good nurture, wheresoever you come.
Now I pray you take good heed,

For this you must know nede, (needs)
But much more you must wyten, (know)
Than you find here written.
If thee fail thereto wit,
Pray to God to send thee it:
For Christ himself, he teacheth ous (us)
That holy church is God's house,
That is made for nothing ellus (else)
But for to pray in, as the book tellus; (tells us)
There the people shall gather in,
To pray and weep for their sin.
Look thou come not to church late,
For to speak harlotry by the gate;

Then to church when thou dost fare,
Have in thy mind ever mare (more)
To worship thy lord God both day and night,
With all thy wits and even thy might.
To the church door when thou dost come
Of that holy water there some thou nome, (take)
For every drop thou feelest there
Quencheth a venial sin, be thou ser. (sure)
But first thou must do down thy hood,
For his love that died on the rood.
Into the church when thou dost gon, (go)
Pull up thy heart to Christ, anon;

Upon the rood thou look up then,
And kneel down fair upon thy knen, (knees)
Then pray to him so here to worche (work)
After the law of holy church,
For to keep the commandments ten,

Regius Manuscript (Modern Text)

That God gave to all men;
And pray to him with mild steven (voice)
To keep thee from the sins seven,
That thou here may, in this life,
Keep thee well from care and strife;
Furthermore he grant thee grace,
In heaven's bliss to have a place.

In holy church leave trifling words
Of lewd speech and foul bordes, (jests)
And put away all vanity,
And say thy pater noster and thine ave;
Look also that thou make no bere, (noise)
But always to be in thy prayer;
If thou wilt not thyself pray,
Hinder no other man by no way.
In that place neither sit nor stand,
But kneel fair down on the ground,
And when the Gospel me read shall,

Fairly thou stand up from the wall,
And bless the fare if that thou can,
When gloria tibi is begun;
And when the gospel is done,
Again thou might kneel down,
On both knees down thou fall,
For his love that bought us all;
And when thou hearest the bell ring
To that holy sakerynge, (sacrament)
Kneel you must both young and old,
And both your hands fair uphold,
And say then in this manner,

Fair and soft without noise;
"Jesu Lord welcome thou be,
In form of bread as I thee see,
Now Jesu for thine holy name,
Shield me from sin and shame;

Shrift and Eucharist thou grant me bo, (both)
Ere that I shall hence go,
And very contrition for my sin,
That I never, Lord, die therein;
And as thou were of maid y-bore (born)
Suffer me never to be y-lore; (lost)
But when I shall hence wend,

Grant me the bliss without end;
Amen! Amen! so mote it be!
Now sweet lady pray for me."
Thus thou might say, or some other thing,
When thou kneelest at the sakerynge. (sacrament)
For covetousness after good, spare thou not
To worship him that all hath wrought;
For glad may a man that day be,
That once in the day may him see;
It is so much worth, without nay, (doubt)
The virtue thereof no man tell may;
But so much good doth that sight,

That Saint Austin telleth full right,
That day thou seest God's body,
Thou shalt have these full securely:-
Meet and drink at thy need,
None that day shalt thou gnede; (lack)
Idle oaths and words bo, (both)
God forgiveth thee also;
Sudden death that same day
Thee dare not dread by no way;
Also that day, I thee plight,
Thou shalt not lose thy eye sight;
And each foot that thou goest then,

That holy sight for to sen, (see)
They shall be told to stand instead,
When thou hast thereto great need;
That messenger the angel Gabriel,

Regius Manuscript (Modern Text)

Will keep them to thee full well.
From this matter now I may pass,
To tell more benefits of the mass:
To church come yet, if thou may,
And hear the mass each day;
If thou may not come to church,
Where that ever thou dost worche, (work)
When thou hearest the mass knylle, (toll)

Pray to God with heart still,
To give they part of that service,
That in church there done is.
Furthermore yet, I will you preach
To your fellows, it for to teach,
When thou comest before a lord,
In hall, in bower, or at the board,
Hood or cap that thou off do,
Ere thou come him entirely to;
Twice or thrice, without doubt,
To that lord thou must lowte; (bow)
With thy right knee let it be do, (done)

Thine own worship thou save so.
Hold off thy cap and hood also,
Till thou have leave it on to do. (put)
All the time thou speakest with him,
Fair and amiably hold up thy chin;
So after the nurture of the book,
In his face kindly thou look.
Foot and hand thou keep full still,
For clawing and tripping, is skill;
From spitting and sniffling keep thee also,
By private expulsion let it go,
And if that thou be wise and felle, (discrete)

Thou has great need to govern thee well.
Into the hall when thou dost wend,
Amongst the gentles, good and hende, (courteous)

Ancient Manuscripts of the Freemasons

Presume not too high for nothing,
For thine high blood, nor thy cunning,
Neither to sit nor to lean,
That is nurture good and clean.
Let not thy countenance therefore abate,
Forsooth good nurture will save thy state.
Father and mother, whatsoever they be,
Well is the child that well may thee,
In hall, in chamber, where thou dost gon; (go)

Good manners make a man.
To the next degree look wisely,
To do them reverence by and by;
Do them yet no reverence all o-rowe, (in turn)
Unless that thou do them know.
To the meat when thou art set,
Fair and honestly thou eat it;
First look that thine hands be clean,
And that thy knife be sharp and keen,
And cut thy bread all at thy meat,
Right as it may be there y-ete. (eaten)
If thou sit by a worthier man,

Then thy self thou art one,
Suffer him first to touch the meat,
Ere thyself to it reach.
To the fairest morsel thou might not strike,
Though that thou do it well like;
Keep thine hands fair and well,
From foul smudging of thy towel;
Thereon thou shalt not thy nose smite. (blow)
Nor at the meat thy tooth thou pike; (pick)
Too deep in cup thou might not sink,
Though thou have good will to drink,
Lest thine eyes would water thereby-

Then were it no courtesy.
Look in thy mouth there be no meat,

Regius Manuscript (Modern Text)

When thou beginnest to drink or speak.
When thou seest any man drinking,
That taketh heed to thy carpynge, (speech)
Soon anon thou cease thy tale,
Whether he drink wine or ale,
Look also thou scorn no man,
In what degree thou seest him gone;
Nor thou shalt no man deprave,
If thou wilt thy worship save;
For such word might there outburst.

That might make thee sit in evil rest.
Close thy hand in thy fist,
And keep thee well from "had I known".
In chamber, among the ladies bright,
Hold thy tongue and spend thy sight;
Laugh thou not with no great cry,
Nor make no lewd sport and ribaldry.
Play thou not but with thy peers,
Nor tell thou not all that thou hears;
Discover thou not thine own deed,
For no mirth, nor for no mede: (reward)
With fair speech thou might have thy will,
With it thou might thy self spylle. (spoil)

When thou meetest a worthy man,
Cap and hood thou hold not on;
In church, in market, or in the gate,
Do him reverence after his state.
If thou goest with a worthier man
Then thyself thou art one,
Let thy foremost shoulder follow his back,
For that is nurture without lack;
When he doth speak, hold thee still,
When he hath done, say for thy will,
In thy speech that thou be felle, (discreet)
And what thou sayest consider thee well;
But deprive thou not him his tale,

Neither at the wine nor at the ale.
Christ then of his high grace,
Save you both wit and space,
Well this book to know and read,
Heaven to have for your mede. (reward)
Amen! Amen! so mote it be!
So say we all for charity.

Regius Manuscript
(The Halliwell Manuscript)
A Poem of Moral Duties
circa 1390
Original and Modern Text

(Original Text)

Hic incipiunt constituciones artis gemetriae secundum Eucyldem.

Whose wol bothe wel rede and loke,
He may fynde wryte yn olde boke
Of grete lordys and eke ladyysse,
That hade mony chyldryn y-fere, y-wisse;
And hade no rentys to fynde hem wyth,
Nowther yn towne, ny felde, ny fryth:
A cownsel togeder they cowthe hem take;
To ordeyne for these chyldryn sake,
How they my[g]th best lede here lyfe
Withoute gret desese, care and stryfe;
And most for the multytude that was comynge
Of here chyldryn after here [g]lyndynge.
(They) sende thenne after grete clerkys,
To techyn hem thenne gode werkys;

And pray we hem, for our Lordys sake,
To oure chyldryn sum werke to make,
That they my[g]th gete here lyvynge therby,

Regius Manuscript (Original Text)

Bothe wel and onestlyche, ful sycurly.
Yn that tyme, thro[g]gh good gemetry,
Thys onest craft of good masonry
Wes ordeynt and made yn thys manere,
Y-cownterfetyd of thys clerkys y-fere;
At these lordys prayers they cownterfetyd
gemetry,
And [g]af hyt the name of masonry,
For the moste oneste craft of alle.
These lordys chyldryn therto dede falle,
To lurne of hym the craft of gemetry,
The wheche he made ful curysly;

Thro[g]gh fadrys prayers and modrys also,
Thys onest craft he putte hem to.
He that lerned best, and were of onesté,
And passud hys felows yn curysté;
[G]ef yn that craft he dede hym passe,
He schulde have more worschepe then the lasse.
Thys grete clerkys name was clept Euclyde,
Hys name hyt spradde ful wondur wyde.
Get thys grete clerke more ordeynt he
To hym that was herre yn thys degré,
That he schulde teche the synplyst of (wytte)
Yn that onest craft to be parfytte;
And so uchon schulle techyn othur,
And love togeder as syster and brothur.

Forthermore [g]et that ordeynt he,
Mayster y-called so schulde he be;
So that he were most y-worschepede,
Thenne sculde he be so y-clepede:
But mason schulde never won other calle,
Withynne the craft amongus hem alle,
Ny soget, ny servand, my dere brother,
Tha[g]ht he be not so perfyt as ys another;
Uchon sculle calle other felows by cuthe,
For cause they come of ladyes burthe.

On thys maner, thro[g] good wytte of gemetry,
Bygan furst the craft of masonry:
The clerk Euclyde on thys wyse hyt fonde,
Thys craft of gemetry yn Egypte londe.

Yn Egypte he taw[g]hte hyt ful wyde,
Yn dyvers londe on every syde;
Mony erys afterwarde, y understonde,
[G]er that the craft com ynto thys londe,
Thys craft com ynto Englond, as y [g]ow say,
Yn tyme of good kynge Adelstonus day;
He made tho bothe halle and eke bowre,
And hye templus of gret honowre,
To sportyn hym yn bothe day and ny[g]th,
An to worschepe hys God with alle hys my[g]th.
Thys goode lorde loved thys craft ful wel,
And purposud to strenthyn hyt every del,
For dyvers defawtys that yn the craft he fonde;
He sende about ynto the londe

After alle the masonus of the crafte,
To come to hym ful evene stra[g]fte,
For to amende these defautys alle
By good consel, [g]ef hyt myt[g]th falle.
A semblé thenne he cowthe let make
Of dyvers lordis, yn here state,
Dukys, erlys, and barnes also,
Kyn[g]thys, sqwyers, and mony mo,
And the grete burges of that syté,
They were ther alle yn here degré;
These were ther uchon algate,
To ordeyne for these masonus astate.
Ther they sow[g]ton by here wytte,
How they my[g]thyn governe hytte:

Fyftene artyculus they ther sow[g]ton
And fyftene poyntys they wro[g]ton.

Regius Manuscript (Original Text)

Hic incipit articulus primus.

The furste artycul of thys gemetry:--
The mayster mason moste be ful securly
Bothe stedefast, trusty, and trwe,
Hyt schal hum never thenne arewe:
And pay thy felows after the coste,
As vytaylys goth thenne, wel thou woste;
And pay them trwly, apon thy fay,
What that they deserven may;
And to her hure take no more,
But what they mowe serve fore;
And spare, nowther for love ny drede,

Of nowther partys to take no mede;
Of lord ny felow, whether he be,
Of hem thou take no maner of fe;
And as a jugge stonde upry[g]th,
And thenne thou dost to bothe good ry[g]th;
And trwly do thys whersever thou gost,
Thy worschep, thy profyt, hyt shcal be most.

Articulus secundus.

The secunde artycul of good masonry,
As [g]e mowe hyt here hyr specyaly,
That every mayster, that ys a mason,
Most ben at the generale congregacyon,
So that he hyt resonably y-tolde
Where that the semblé schal be holde;

And to that semblé he most nede gon,
But he have a resenabul skwsacyon,
Or but he be unbuxom to that craft,
Or with falssehed ys over-raft,
Or ellus sekenes hath hym so stronge,
That he may not com hem amonge;
That ys a skwsacyon, good and abulle,

To that semblé withoute fabulle.

Articulus tercius.

The thrydde artycul for sothe hyt ysse,
That the mayster take to no prentysse,
but he have good seuerans to dwelle
Seven [g]er with hym, as y [g]ow telle,
Hys craft to lurne, that ys profytable;

Withynne lasse he may not be able
To lordys profyt, ny to his owne,
As [g]e mowe knowe by good resowne.

Articulus quartus.

The fowrhe artycul thys moste be
That the mayster hym wel be-se,
That he no bondemon prentys make,
Ny for no covetyse do hym take;
For the lord that he ys bonde to,
May fache the prentes whersever he go.
Gef yn the logge he were y-take,
Muche desese hyt mygth ther make,
And suche case hyt mygth befalle,
That hyt mygth greve summe or alle.

For alle the masonus tht ben there
Wol stonde togedur hol y-fere
Gef suche won yn that craft schulde swelle,
Of dyvers desesys ge mygth telle:
For more gese thenne, and of honeste,
Take a prentes of herre degre.
By olde tyme wryten y fynde
That the prenes schulde be of gentyl kynde;
And so symtyme grete lordys blod
Toke thys gemetry, that ys ful good.

Regius Manuscript (Original Text)

Articulus quintus.

The fyfthe artycul ys swythe good,
So that the prentes be of lawful blod;
The mayster schal not, for no vantage,

Make no prentes that ys outrage;
Hyt ys to mene, as [g]e mowe here,
That he have hys lymes hole alle y-fere;
To the craft hyt were gret schame,
To make an halt mon and a lame,
For an unperfyt mon of suche blod
Schulde do the craft but lytul good.
Thus [g]e mowe knowe everychon,
The craft wolde have a my[g]hty mon;
A maymed mon he hath no my[g]ht,
[G]e mowe hyt knowe long [g]er ny[g]ht.

Articulus sextus.

The syxte artycul [g]e mowe not mysse,

That the mayster do the lord no pregedysse,
To take of the lord, for hyse prentyse,
Also muche as hys felows don, yn alle vyse.
For yn that craft they ben ful perfyt,
So ys not he, [g]e mowe sen hyt.
Also hyt were a[g]eynus good reson,
To take hys, hure as hys felows don.
Thys same artycul, yn thys casse,
Juggythe the prentes to take lasse
Thenne hys felows, that ben ful perfyt.
Yn dyvers maters, conne qwyte hyt,
The mayster may his prentes so enforme,
That hys hure may crese ful [g]urne,

And, ger hys terme come to an ende,
Hys hure may ful wel amende.

Articulus septimus.

The seventhe artycul that ys now here,
Ful wel wol telle gow, alle y-fere,
That no mayster, for favour ny drede,
Schal no thef nowther clothe ny fede.
Theves he schal herberon never won,
Ny hym that hath y-quellude a mon,
Wy thylike that hath a febul name,
Lest hyt wolde turne the craft to schame.

Articulus octavus.

The eghte artycul schewt [g]ow so,

That the mayster may hyt wel do,
[G]ef that he have any mon of crafte,
And be not also perfyt as he au[g]te,
He may hym change sone anon,
And take for hym a perfytur mon.
Suche a mon, thro[g]e rechelaschepe,
My[g]th do the craft schert worschepe.

Articulus nonus.

The nynthe artycul schewet ful welle,
That the mayster be both wyse and felle;
That no werke he undurtake,
But he conne bothe hyt ende and make;
And that hyt be to the lordes profyt also,

And to hys craft, whersever he go;
And that the grond be wel y-take,
That hyt nowther fle ny grake.

Articulus decimus.

The then the artycul ys for to knowe,

Regius Manuscript (Original Text)

Amonge the craft, to hye and lowe,
There schal no mayster supplante other,
But be togeder as systur and brother,
Yn thys curyus craft, alle and som,
That longuth to a maystur mason.
Ny he schal not supplante non other mon,
That hath y-take a werke hym uppon,
Yn peyne therof that ys so stronge,

That peyseth no lasse thenne ten ponge,
But [g]ef that he be gulty y-fonde,
That toke furst the werke on honde;
For no mon yn masonry
Schal no supplante othur securly,
But [g]ef that hyt be so y-wro[g]th,
That hyt turne the werke to nogth;
Thenne may a mason that werk crave,
To the lordes profyt hyt for to save;
Yn suche a case but hyt do falle,
Ther schal no mason medul withalle.
Forsothe he that begynnyth the gronde,
And he be a mason goode and sonde,
For hath hyt sycurly yn hys mynde

To brynge the werke to ful good ende.

Articulus undecimus.

The eleventhe artycul y telle the,
That he ys bothe fayr and fre;
For he techyt, by hys my[g]th,
That no mason schulde worche be ny[g]th,
But [g]ef hyt be yn practesynge of wytte,
[G]ef that y cowthe amende hytte.

Articulus duodecimus.

The twelfthe artycul ys of hye honesté

To [g]every mason, whersever he be;
He schal not hys felows werk deprave,
[G]ef that he wol hys honesté save;
With honest wordes he hyt comende,

By the wytte that God the dede sende;
Buy hyt amende by al that thou may,
Bytwynne [g]ow bothe withoute nay.

Articulus xiijus.

The threttene artycul, so God me save,
Ys,[g]ef that the mayster a prentes have,
Enterlyche thenne that he hym teche,
And meserable poyntes that he hym reche,
That he the craft abelyche may conne,
Whersever he go undur the sonne.

Articulus xiiijus.

The fowrtene artycul, by good reson,
Scheweth the mayster how he schal don;
He schal no prentes to hym take,

Byt dyvers crys he have to make,
That he may, withynne hys terme,
Of hym dyvers poyntes may lurne.

Articulus quindecimus.

The fyftene artycul maketh an ende,
For to the mayster he ys a frende;
To lere hym so, that for no mon,
No fals mantenans he take hym apon,
Ny maynteine hys felows yn here synne,
For no good that he my[g]th wynne;
Ny no fals sware sofre hem to make,
For drede of here sowles sake;

Regius Manuscript (Original Text)

Lest hyt wolde turne the craft to schame,
And hymself to mechul blame.

Plures Constituciones.

At thys semblé were poyntes y-ordeynt mo,
Of grete lordys and maystrys also,
That whose wol conne thys craft and com to astate,
He most love wel God, and holy churche algate,
And hys mayster also, that he ys wythe,
Whersever he go, yn fylde or frythe;
And thy felows thou love also,
For that they craft wol that thou do.

Secundus punctus.

The secunde poynt, as y [g]ow say,
That the mason worche apon the werk day,
Also trwly, as he con or may,

To deserve hys huyre for the halyday,
And trwly to labrun on hys dede,
Wel deserve to have hys mede.

Tercius punctus.

The thrydde poynt most be severele,
With the prentes knowe hyt wele,
Hys mayster conwsel he kepe and close,
And hys felows by hys goode purpose;
The prevetyse of the chamber telle he no man,
Ny yn the logge whatsever they done;
Whatsever thou heryst, or syste hem do,
Telle hyt no mon, whersever thou go;
The conwsel of halls, and [g]eke of bowre,

Kepe hyt wel to gret honowre,

Lest hyt wolde torne thyself to blame,
And brynge the craft ynto gret schame.

Quartus punctus.

The fowrthe poynt techyth us alse,
That no mon to hys craft be false;
Errour he schal maynteine none
A[g]eynus the craft, but let hyt gone;
Ny no pregedysse he schal not do
To hys mayster, ny hys felows also;
And that[g]th the prentes be under awe,
[G]et he wolde have the same lawe.

Quintus punctus.

The fyfthe poynte ys, withoute nay,
That whenne the mason taketh hys pay
Of the mayster, y-ordent to hym,
Ful mekely y-take so most hyt byn;
[G]et most the mayster, by good resone,
Warne hem lawfully byfore none,
[G]ef he nulle okepye hem no more,
As he hath y-done ther byfore;
A[g]eynus thys ordyr he may not stryve,
[G]ef he thenke wel for to thryve.

Sextus punctus.

The syxte poynt ys ful [g]ef to knowe,
Bothe to hye and eke to lowe,

For suche case hyt my[g]th befalle,
Amonge the masonus, summe or alle,
Throwghe envye, or dedly hate,
Ofte aryseth ful gret debate.
Thenne owyth the mason, [g]ef that he may,
Putte hem bothe under a day;

Regius Manuscript (Original Text)

But loveday [g]et schul they make none;
Tyl that the werke day be clene a-gone;
Apon the holyday [g]e mowe wel take
Leyser y-now[g]gth loveday to make,
Lest that hyt wolde the werke day
Latte here werke for suche afray;
To suche ende thenne that hem drawe,

That they stonde wel yn Goddes lawe.

Septimus punctus.

The seventhe poynt he may wel mene,
Of wel longe lyf that God us lene,
As hyt dyscryeth wel opunly,
Thou schal not by thy maysters wyf ly,
Ny by the felows, yn no maner wyse,
Lest the craft wolde the despyse;
Ny by the felows concubyne,
No more thou woldest he dede by thyne.
The peyne thereof let hyt be ser,
That he prentes ful seven [g]er,
[G]ef he forfete yn eny of hem,

So y-chasted thenne most he ben;
Ful mekele care my[g]th ther begynne,
For suche a fowle dedely synne.

Octavus punctus.

The eghte poynt, he may be sure,
[G]ef thou hast y-taken any cure,
Under thy mayster thou be trwe,
For that pynt thou schalt never arewe;
A trwe medyater thou most nede be
To thy mayster, and thy felows fre;
Do trwly al....that thou my[g]th,
To both partyes, and that ys good ry[g]th.

Nonus punctus.

The nynthe poynt we schul hym calle,
That he be stwarde of oure halle,
Gef that ge ben yn chambur y-fere,
Uchon serve other, with mylde chere;
Jentul felows, ge moste hyt knowe,
For to be stwardus alle o rowe,
Weke after weke withoute dowte,
Stwardus to ben so alle abowte,
Lovelyche to serven uchon othur,
As thawgh they were syster and brother;
Ther schal never won on other costage
Fre hymself to no vantage,
But every mon schal be lyche fre

Yn that costage, so moste hyt be;
Loke that thou pay wele every mon algate,
That thou hsat y-bow[g]ht any vytayles ate,
That no cravynge be y-mad to the,
Ny to thy felows, yn no degré,
To mon or to wommon, whether he be,
Pay hem wel and trwly, for that wol we;
Therof on thy felow trwe record thou take,
For that good pay as thou dost make,
Lest hyt wolde thy felowe schame,
Any brynge thyself ynto gret blame.
[G]et good acowntes he most make
Of suche godes as he hath y-take,

Of thy felows goodes that thou hast spende,
Wher, and how, and to what ende;
Suche acowntes thou most come to,
Whenne thy felows wollen that thou do.

Decimus punctus.

The tenthe poynt presentyeth wel god lyf,

To lyven withoute care and stryf;
For and the mason lyve amysse,
And yn hys werk be false, y-wysse,
And thorw[g] suche a false skewysasyon
May sclawndren hys felows oute reson,
Throw[g] false sclawnder of suche fame

May make the craft kachone blame.
[G]ef he do the craft suche vylany,
Do hym no favour thenne securly.
Ny maynteine not hym yn wyked lyf,
Lest hyt wolde turne to care and stryf;
But get hym [g]e schul not delayme,
But that [g]e schullen hym constrayne,
For to apere whersevor [g]e wylle,
Whar that [g]e wolen, lowde, or stylle;
To the nexte semblé [g]e schul hym calle,
To apere byfore hys felows alle,
And but [g]ef he wyl byfore hem pere,

The crafte he moste nede forswere;
He schal thenne be chasted after the lawe
That was y-fownded by olde dawe.

Punctus undecimus.

The eleventhe poynt ys of good dyscrecyoun,
As [g]e mowe knowe by good resoun;
A mason, and he thys craft wel con,
That sy[g]th hys felow hewen on a ston,
And ys yn poynt to spylle that ston,
Amende hyt sone, [g]ef that thou con,
And teche hym thenne hyt to amende,
That the l(ordys) werke be not y-schende,
And teche hym esely hyt to amende,

With fayre wordes, that God the hath lende;
For hys sake that sytte above,

With swete wordes noresche hym love.

Punctus duodecimus.

The twelthe poynt of gret ryolté,
Ther as the semblé y-hole schal be,
Ther schul be maystrys and felows also,
And other grete lordes mony mo;
There schal be the scheref of that contré,
And also the meyr of that syté,
Kny[g]tes and sqwyers ther schul be,
And other aldermen, as [g]e schul se;
Suche ordynance as they maken there,

They schul maynté hyt hol y-fere
A[g]eynus that mon, whatsever he be,
That longuth to the craft bothe fayr and fre.
[G]ef he any stryf a[g]eynus hem make,
Ynto here warde he schal be take.

xiijus punctus.

The threnteth poynt ys to us ful luf.
He schal swere never to be no thef,
Ny soker hym yn hys fals craft,
For no good that he hath byraft,
And thou mowe hyt knowe or syn,
Nowther for hys good, ny for hys kyn.

xiiijus punctus.

The fowrtethe poynt ys ful good lawe
To hym that wold ben under awe;
A good trwe othe he most ther swere
To hys mayster and hys felows that ben there;
He most be stedefast and trwe also
To alle thys ordynance, whersever he go,
And to hys lyge lord the kynge,

Regius Manuscript (Original Text)

To be trwe to hym, over alle thynge.
And alle these poyntes hyr before
To hem thou most nede by y-swore,
And alle schul swere the same ogth
Of the masonus, be they luf, ben they loght,
To alle these poyntes hyr byfore,

That hath ben ordeynt by ful good lore.
And they schul enquere every mon
On his party, as wyl as he con,
[G]ef any mon mowe be y-fownde gulty
Yn any of these poyntes spesyaly;
And whad he be, let hym be sow[g]ht,
And to the semblé let hym be brow[g]ht.

Quindecimus punctus.

The fiftethe poynt ys of ful good lore,
For hem that schul ben ther y-swore,
Suche ordyance at the semblé wes layd
Of grete lordes and maystres byforesayd;
For thelke that be unbuxom, y-wysse,

A[g]eynus the ordynance that ther ysse
Of these artyculus, that were y-meved there,
Of grete lordes and masonus al y-fere.
And [g]ef they ben y-preved opunly
Byfore that semblé, by an by,
And for here gultes no mendys wol make,
Thenne most they nede the crafy forsake;
And so masonus craft they schul refuse,
And swere hyt never more for to use.
But [g]ef that they wol mendys make,
A[g]ayn to the craft they schul never take;
And [g]ef that they nul not do so,
The scheref schal come hem sone to,

And putte here bodyes yn duppe prison,

For the trespasse that they hav y-don,
And take here goodes and here cattelle
Ynto the kynges hond, everyt delle,
And lete hem dwelle ther full stylle,
Tyl hyt be oure lege kynges wylle.

Alia ordinacio artis gematriae.

They ordent ther a semblé to be y-holde
Every [g]er, whersever they wolde,
To amende the defautes, [g]ef any where fonde
Amonge the craft withynne the londe;
Uche [g]er or thrydde [g]er hyt schuld be holde,

Yn every place whersever they wolde;
Tyme and place most be ordeynt also,
Yn what place they schul semble to.
Alle the men of craft tehr they most ben,
And other grete lordes, as [g]e mowe sen,
To mende the fautes that buth ther y-spoke,
[G]ef that eny of hem ben thenne y-broke.
Ther they schullen ben alle y-swore,
That longuth to thys craftes lore,
To kepe these statutes everychon,
That ben y-ordeynt by kynge Aldelston;
These statutes that y have hyr y-fonde

Y chulle they ben holde thro[g]h my londe,
For the worsche of my ry[g]olté,
That y have by my dygnyté.
Also at every semblé that [g]e holde,
That ge come to [g]owre lyge kyng bolde,
Bysechynge hym of hys hye grace,
To stonde with [g]ow yn every place,
To conferme the statutes of kynge Adelston,
That he ordeydnt to thys craft by good reson,

Regius Manuscript (Original Text)

Ars quatuor coronatorum.

Pray we now to God almy[g]ht,
And to hys moder Mary bry[g]ht,

That we mowe keepe these artyculus here,
And these poynts wel al y-fere,
As dede these holy martyres fowre,
That yn thys craft were of gret honoure;
They were as gode masonus as on erthe schul go,
Gravers and ymage-makers they were also.
For they were werkemen of the beste,
The emperour hade to hem gret luste;
He wylned of hem a ymage to make,
That mow[g]h be worscheped for his sake;
Suche mawmetys he hade yn hys dawe,
To turne the pepul from Crystus lawe.

But they were stedefast yn Crystes lay,
And to here craft, withouten nay;
They loved wel God and alle hys lore,
And weren yn hys serves ever more.
Trwe men they were yn that dawe,
And lyved wel y Goddus lawe;
They tho[g]ght no mawmetys for to make,
For no good that they my[g]th take,
To levyn on that mawmetys for here God,
They nolde do so thaw[g] he were wod;
For they nolde not forsake here trw fay,

An beyleve on hys falsse lay.
The emperour let take hem sone anone,
And putte hem ynto a dep presone;
The sarre he penest hem yn that plase,
The more yoye wes to hem of Cristus grace.
Thenne when he sye no nother won,
To dethe he lette hem thenne gon;
Whose wol of here lyf [g]et mor knowe,

By the bok he may kyt schowe,
In the legent of scanctorum,
The name of quatour coronatorum.

Here fest wol be, withoute nay,
After Alle Halwen the eyght day.
[G]e mow here as y do rede,
That mony [g]eres after, for gret drede
That Noees flod wes alle y-ronne,
The tower of Babyloyne was begonne,
Also playne werke of lyme and ston,
As any mon schulde loke uppon;
So long and brod hyt was begonne,
Seven myle the he[g]ghte schadweth the sonne.
King Nabogodonosor let hyt make,
To gret strenthe for monus sake,

Tha[g]gh suche a flod a[g]ayne schulde come,
Over the werke hyt schulde not nome;
For they hadde so hy pride, with stronge bost,
Alle that werke therfore was y-lost;
An angele smot hem so with dyveres speche,
That never won wyste what other schuld reche.
Mony eres after, the goode clerk Euclyde
Ta[g]ghte the craft of gemetré wonder wyde,
So he ded that tyme other also,
Of dyvers craftes mony mo.
Thro[g]gh hye grace of Crist yn heven,
He commensed yn the syens seven;

Gramatica ys the furste syens y-wysse,
Dialetica the secunde, so have y blysse,
Rethorica the thrydde, withoute nay,
Musica ys the fowrth, as y [g]ow say,
Astromia ys the v, by my snowte,
Arsmetica the vi, withoute dowte
Gemetria the seventhe maketh an ende,
For he ys bothe make and hende,

Regius Manuscript (Original Text)

Gramer forsothe ys the rote,
Whose wyl lurne on the boke;
But art passeth yn hys degré,
As the fryte doth the rote of the tre;

Rethoryk metryth with orne speche amonge,
And musyke hyt ys a swete song;
Astronomy nombreth, my dere brother,
Arsmetyk scheweth won thyng that ys another,
Gemetré the seventh syens hyt ysse,
That con deperte falshed from trewthe y-wys.
These bene the syens seven,
Whose useth hem wel, he may han heven.
Now dere chyldren, by [g]owre wytte,
Pride and covetyse that [g]e leven, hytte,
And taketh hede to goode dyscrecyon,
And to good norter, whersever [g]e com.
Now y pray [g]ow take good hede,

For thys [g]e most kenne nede,
But much more [g]e moste wyten,
Thenne [g]e fynden hyr y-wryten.
[G]ef the fayle therto wytte,
Pray to God to send the hytte;
For Crist hymself, he techet ous
That holy churche ys Goddes hous,
That ys y-mad for nothynge ellus
but for to pray yn, as the bok tellus;
Ther the pepul schal gedur ynne,
To pray and wepe for here synne.
Loke thou come not to churche late,
For to speke harlotry by the gate;

Thenne to churche when thou dost fare,
Have yn thy mynde ever mare
To worschepe thy lord God bothe day and ny[g]th,
With all thy wyttes, and eke thy my[g]th.
To the churche dore when tou dost come,

Of that holy water ther sum thow nome,
For every drope thou felust ther
Qwenchet a venyal synne, be thou ser.
But furst thou most do down thy hode,
For hyse love that dyed on the rode.
Into the churche when thou dost gon,
Pulle uppe thy herte to Crist, anon;

Uppon the rode thou loke uppe then,
And knele down fayre on bothe thy knen;
Then pray to hym so hyr to worche,
After the lawe of holy churche,
For to kepe the comandementes ten,
That God [g]af to alle men;
And pray to hym with mylde steven
To kepe the from the synnes seven,
That thou hyr mowe, yn thy lyve,
Kepe the wel from care and stryve,
Forthermore he grante the grace,
In heven blysse to hav a place.

In holy churche lef nyse wordes
Of lewed speche, and fowle bordes,
And putte away alle vanyté,
And say thy pater noster and thyn ave;
Loke also thou make no bere,
But ay to be yn thy prayere;
[G]ef thou wolt not thyselve pray,
Latte non other mon by no way.
In that place nowther sytte ny stonde,
But knele fayre down on the gronde,
And, when the Gospel me rede schal,

Fayre thou stonde up fro the wal,
And blesse the fayre, [g]ef that thou conne,
When gloria tibi is begonne;
And when the gospel ys y-done,
A[g]ayn thou my[g]th knele adown;

Regius Manuscript (Original Text)

On bothe thy knen down thou falle,
For hyse love that bow[g]ht us alle;
And when thou herest the belle rynge
To that holy sakerynge,
Knele [g]e most, bothe [g]yn[g]e and olde,
And bothe [g]or hondes fayr upholde,
And say thenne yn thys manere,

Fayr and softe, withoute bere;
"Jhesu Lord, welcom thou be,
Yn forme of bred, as y the se.
Now Jhesu, for thyn holy name,
Schulde me from synne and schame,
Schryff and hosel thou grant me bo,
[G]er that y schal hennus go,
And vey contrycyon of my synne,
Tath y never, Lord, dye therynne;
And, as thou were of a mayde y-bore,
Sofre me never to be y-lore;
But when y schal hennus wende,

Grante me the blysse withoute ende;
Amen! amen! so mot hyt be!
Now, swete lady, pray for me."
Thus thou my[g]ht say, or sum other thynge,
When thou knelust at the sakerynge.
For covetyse after good, spare thou nought
To worschepe hym that alle hath wrought;
For glad may a mon that day ben,
That onus yn the day may hym sen;
Hyt ys so muche worthe, withoute nay,
The vertu therof no mon telle may;
But so meche good doth that syht,

As seynt Austyn telluth ful ryht,
That day thou syst Goddus body,
Thou schalt have these, ful securly:-
Mete and drynke at thy nede,

Non that day schal the gnede;
Ydul othes, an wordes bo,
God for[g]eveth the also;
Soden deth, that ylke day,
The dar not drede by no way;
Also that day, y the plyht,
Thou schalt not lese thy eye syht;
And uche fote that thou gost then,

That holy syht for to sen,
They schul be told to stonde yn stede,
When thou hast therto gret nede;
That messongere, the angele Gabryelle,
Wol kepe hem to the ful welle.
From thys mater now y may passe,
To telle mo medys of the masse:
To churche come [g]et, [g]ef thou may,
And here thy masse uche day;
[G]ef thou mowe not come to churche,
Wher that ever thou doste worche,
When thou herest to masse knylle,

Pray to God with herte stylle,
To [g]eve the part of that servyse,
That yn churche ther don yse.
Forthermore [g]et, y wol [g]ow preche
To [g]owre felows, hyt for to teche,
When thou comest byfore a lorde,
Yn halle, yn bowre, or at the borde,
Hod or cappe that thou of do,
[G]er thou come hym allynge to;
Twyes or thryes, without dowte,
To that lord thou moste lowte;
With thy ry[g]th kne let hyt be do,

Thyn owne worschepe tou save so.
Holde of thy cappe, and hod also,
Tyl thou have leve hyt on to do.

Regius Manuscript (Original Text)

Al the whyle thou spekest with hym,
Fayre and lovelyche bere up thy chyn;
So, after the norter of the boke,
Yn hys face lovely thou loke.
Fot and hond, thou kepe ful stylle
From clawynge and trypynge, ys sckylle;
From spyttynge and snyftynge kepe the also,
By privy avoydans let hyt go.
And [g]ef that thou be wyse and felle,

Thou hast gret nede to governe the welle.
Ynto the halle when thou dost wende,
Amonges the genteles, good and hende,
Presume not to hye for nothynge,
For thyn hye blod, ny thy connynge,
Nowther to sytte, ny to lene,
That ys norther good and clene.
Let not thy cowntenans therfore abate,
Forsothe, good norter wol save thy state.
Fader and moder, whatsever they be,
Wel ys the chyld that wel may the,
Yn halle, yn chamber, wher thou dost gon;

Gode maneres maken a mon.
To the nexte degré loke wysly,
To do hem reverans by and by;
Do hem [g]et no reverans al o-rowe,
But [g]ef that thou do hem know.
To the mete when thou art y-sette,
Fayre and onestelyche thou ete hytte;
Fyrst loke that thyn honden be clene,
And that thy knyf be scharpe and kene;
And kette thy bred al at thy mete,
Ry[g]th as hyt may be ther y-ete.
[G]ef thou sytte by a worththyur mon.

Then thy selven thou art won,
Sofre hym fyrst to toyche the mete,

[G]er thyself to hyt reche.
To the fayrest mossel thou my[g]ht not strike,
Thaght that thou do hyt wel lyke;
Kepe thyn hondes, fayr and wel,
From fowle smogynge of thy towel;
Theron thou schalt not thy nese snyte,
Ny at the mete thy tothe thou pyke;
To depe yn the coppe thou my[g]ght not synke,
Thagh thou have good wyl to drynke,
Lest thyn enyn wolde wattryn therby_

Then were hyt no curtesy
Loke yn thy mowth ther be no mete,
When thou begynnyst to drynke or speke.
When thou syst any mon drynkynge,
That taketh hed to thy carpynge,
Sone anonn thou sese thy tale,
Whether he drynke wyn other ale.
Loke also thou scorne no mon,
Yn what degré thou syst hym gon;
Ny thou schalt no mon deprave,
[G]ef thou wolt thy worschepe save;
For suche worde my[g]ht ther outberste,

That myg[h]t make the sytte yn evel reste,
Close thy honde yn thy fyste,
And kepe the wel from "had-y-wyste."
Yn chamber amonge the ladyes bryght,
Holde thy tonge and spende thy syght;
Law[g]e thou not with no gret cry,
Ny make no ragynge with rybody.
Play thou not buyt with thy peres,
Ny tel thou not al that thou heres;
Dyskever thou not thyn owne dede,
For no merthe, ny for no mede;
With fayr speche thou myght have thy wylle,
With hyt thou myght thy selven spylle.

Regius Manuscript (Original Text)

When thou metyst a worthy mon,
Cappe and hod thou holle not on;
Yn churche, yn chepyns, or yn the gate,
Do hym revera(n)s after hys state.
[G]ef thou gost with a worthyor mon
Then thyselven thou art won,
Let thy forther schulder sewe hys backe,
For that ys norter withoute lacke;
When he doth speke, holte the stylle,
When he hath don, sey for thy wylle;
Yn thy speche that thou be felle,
And what thou sayst avyse the welle;
But byref thou not hym hys tale,
Nowther at the wyn, ny at the ale.
Cryst then of hys hye grace,
[G]eve [g]ow bothe wytte and space,
Wel thys boke to conne and rede,
Heven to have for [g]owre mede.
Amen! amen! so mot hyt be!
Say we so all per charyté.

The Matthew Cooke Manuscript
circa 1450

Thanked be God, our glorious Father, the founder and creator of heaven and earth, and of all things that therein are, for that he has vouchsafed, of his glorious Godhead, to make so many things of manifold virtue for the use of mankind. For he made all things to be subject and obedient to man. All things eatable of a wholesome nature he ordained for man's sustenance. And moreover, he hath given to man wit and the knowledge of divers things and handicrafts, by the which we may labour in this world, in order to therewith get our livelihood and fashion many objects, pleasant in the sight of God, to our own ease and profit. To rehearse all these matters here were too long in the writing or telling, I will therefore refrain; but I will nevertheless, tell you some; for instance, how and in what manner the Science of Geometry was first invented, and who were the founders both thereof and of several other crafts, as is declared in the Bible, and other histories.

How, and in what manner this worthy Science of Geometry took its rise, I will tell you, as I said before. You must know that there are seven liberal sciences, from which seven all other sciences and crafts in the world sprung; but especially is Geometry the first cause of all the other sciences, whatsoevor they be.

These seven sciences are as follows:

The first, which is called the foundation of all science, is grammar, which teacheth to write and speak correctly.

The second is rhetoric, which teaches us to speak elegantly.

The third is dialectic, which teaches us to discern the true from the false, and it is usually called art or sophistry (logic).

The fourth is arithmetic, which instructs us in the science of numbers, to reckon, and to make accounts.

The fifth is Geometry, which teaches us all about mensuration, measures and weights, of all kinds of handicrafts.

The sixth is music, and that teaches the art of singing by notation for the voice, on the organ, trumpet, and harp, and of all things pertaining thereto.

The seventh is astronomy, which teaches us the course of the sun and of the moon and of the other stars and planets of heaven.

Our intent is to treat chiefly of the first foundation of Geometry and who were the founders thereof. As I said before, there are seven liberal sciences, that is to say, seven sciences or crafts that are free in themselves, the which seven exist only through Geometry. And Geometry may be described as earth-mensuration, for Geometry is derived from geo, which is in Greek "earth," and metrona or a measure. Thus is the word Geometry compounded and signifies the measure of the earth.

Marvel not because I said that all sciences exist only through the science of Geometry. For there is no art or handicraft wrought by man's hands that is not wrought by Geometry which is a chief factor (notabulle cause) thereof. For if a man work with his hands he employs some sort of tool, and there is no instrument of any material in this world which is not formed of some sort of earth (ore) and to earth it will return. And there is no instrument or tool to work with that has not some proportion, more or less. And proportion is measure, and the instrument or tool is earth. And Geometry is earth-mensuration therefore I affirm that all men live by Geometry. For all men here to this world live by the labour of their hands.

Many more proofs could I give you that Geometry is the science by which all reasoning men live, but I refrain at this time because the writing of it were a long process.

And now I will enter further into the matter You must know that among all the crafts followed by man in this world, Masonry has the greatest renown end the largest share of this science of Geometry, as is stated in history, such as the Bible, and the Master of History," and in the Policronicon a well authenticated (or trustworthy) chronicle, and in the history called Beda De Imagine Mundi, and Isodorus Ethomolegiarum Methodius Episcopus & Martiris. And many others say that Masonry is the chief part of Geometry and so methinks it may well be said, for it was the first founded, as is stated in the Bible, in the first book of Genesis and the fourth chapter. And moreover all the learned authors above cited agree thereto. And some of them affirm it more openly and plainly, precisely as in Genesis in the Bible.

Before Noah's Flood by direct male descent from Adam in the seventh generation, there lived a man called Lamech who had two wives, called Adah and Zillah. By the first wife, Adah, he begat two sons, Jabal and Jubal. The elder son Jabal was the first man that ever discovered geometry and masonry, and he made houses, and is called in the Bible the father of all men who dwell in tents or dwelling houses. And he was Cain's master mason and governor of the works when he built the city of Enoch, which was the first city ever made and was built by Cain, Adam's son, who gave it to his own son Enoch, and give the city the name of his son and called it Enoch, and now it is known as Ephraim. And at that place was the Science of Geometry and Masonry first prosecuted and contrived as a science and as a handicraft. And so we may well say that it is the first cause and foundation of all crafts and sciences. And also this man Jabel was called the father of shepherds. The Master of History says, and Beda De Imagine Mundi and the Policronicon and many others more say, that he was the first that made partition of lands, in order that every man might know his own land and labour thereon for himself. And also he divided flocks of sheep, that every man might know his own sheep, and so we may say that he was the inventor of that science.

And his brother Jubal or Tubal was the inventor of music and song, as Pythagoras states in Polycronicon, and the same says Isodorous. In his Ethemolegiis in the 6th book he says that he was the first founder of music and song, and of the organ and trumpet; and he discovered that science by the sound of the weights of his brother's, Tubal-Cain's, hammers.

And of a truth, as the Bible says, that is to say, in the fourth Chapter of Genesis, Lamech begat by his other wife Zillah a son and a daughter, and their names Tubal Cain, that was the son, and the daughter was called Naamah. And according to the Policronicon, some men say that she was Noah's wife; but whether this be so or not, we will not affirm.

Ye must know that this son Tubal Cain was the founder of the smith's craft and of other handicrafts dealing with metals, such as iron, brass, gold and silver as some learned writers say; and his sister Naamah discovered the craft of weaving for before her time no cloth was woven, but they span yarn and knit it and made such clothing as they could. And as this woman Naamah invented the craft of weaving it was called woman's-craft.

And these four brethren knew that God would take vengeance for sin, either by fire or water. And they were much concerned how to save the sciences they had discovered, and they took counsel together and exercised all their wits. And they said there were two kinds of stone of such virtue that the one would not burn, called marble, and the other named "Lacerus" would not sink in water. And so they devised to write all the sciences they had found on these two stones, so that if God took vengeance by fire the marble would not burn, and if by water the other would not drown, and they besought their elder brother Jabal to make two pillars of these two stones, that is of marble and of "Lacerus," and to write on the two pillars all the sciences and crafts which they had found and he did so. And therefore we may say that he was the wisest in science, for he first began and carried out their purpose before Noah's flood,

Fortunately knowing of the vengeance that God would send, the brethren knew not whether it would be by fire or water. They knew by a sort of prophecy that God would send one or the other, and therefore they wrote their sciences on the two pillars of stone. And some men say that they wrote on the stones all the seven sciences, but [this I affirm not]. As they had it in mind that a vengeance would come, so it befell that God did send vengeance, and there came such a flood that all the world was drowned and all men died save only eight persons. These were Noah and his wife and his three sons and their wives, of which sons all the world is descended, and they were named in this wise, Shem, Ham and Japhet. And this flood is called Noah's Flood, for he and his children were saved therein. And many years after the flood, according to the chronicle, these two pillars were found, and the chronicle says that a great clerk, Pythagoras, found the one, and Hermes the philosopher found the other, and they taught the sciences that they found written thereon.

Every chronicle and history and many other writers and the Bible especially relate the building or the tower of Babel; and it is written in the Bible, Genesis, Chap. x how that Ham, Noah's son, begat Nimrod, who grew a mighty man upon the earth and waxed strong, like unto a giant. He was a great king and the beginning of his kingdom was the kingdom of Babilon proper, and Erech and Arend and Calnch and the land of Shinar. And this same Ham began the tower of Babel and taught his workmen the Craft of Masonry and he had with him many masons, more than 40,000, and he loved and cherished them well. And it is written in Polycronicon, and in the Master of History, and in other histories, and beyond this the Bible witnesses in the same 10th chapter, as it is written, that Ashur who was of near kindred to Nimrod went forth from the land of Shinar and built the City of Nineveh and Plateas (sic) and many more. For it is written "Do terra illa" [&c.]

It is but reasonable that we should plainly say how and in what manner the Charges of the Mason's Craft were first founded, and who first gave it the name of Masonry And you must know that it is stated and written in the Polycronicon and in Methothus Episcopus and Martiris that Ashur who was a worthy lord of Shinar, sent to Nimrod the king to send him Masons and workmen of the Craft that they might help him make his city which he was minded to make. And Nimrod sent him 3000 masons. And as they were about to depart and go forth, he called them before him and said to them, "Ye must go to my cousin Ashur to help him build a city, but see to it, that ye be well governed, and I will give you a Charge that shall be to your and my profit.

"When you come to that lord, look that you be true to him, even as you would be to me, labour at your Craft honestly, and take a reasonable payment for it such as you may deserve. Love each other as though you were brothers and hold together staunchly. Let him that hath most skill teach his fellow, and be careful that your conduct amongst yourselves and towards your lord may be to my credit, that I may have thanks for sending you and teaching you the Craft." And they received the charge from him, being their lord and master, and went forth to Ashur and built the city of Nineveh in the country of Plateas (sic) and other cities also that are called Calah and Rosen, which is a great city between Calah and Nineveh. And in this manner the Craft of Masonry was first instituted and charged as a science.

Elders of Masons before our times had these charges in writing as we have them now in our Charges of the story of Euclid, and as we have seen them written both in Latin and in French.

But it is only reasonable that we should tell you how Euclid came to the knowledge of Geometry, as stated in the Bible and in other histories. In the XIIth chapter of Genesis it is told how Abraham came to the land of Canaan and our Lord appeared unto him and said, "I will give this land to thy seed." But a great famine reigned in that land and Abraham took Sarah, his wife, with him and made a journey into Egypt to abide there whilst the famine lasted. And Abraham, so says the chronicle, was as a wise man and a learned. And he knew all the seven sciences and taught the Egyptians the science of Geometry. And this worthy clerk Euclid was his pupil and learned of him. And he first gave it the name of Geometry ; although it was practised before his time, it had not acquired the name of Geometry. But it is said by Isodoras in the 5th Book and first Chapter of Ethomolegiarum that Euclid was one of the first founders of Geometry and gave it that name.

For in his time, the river of Egypt which is called the Nile so overflowed the land that no man could dwell therein. Then the worthy clerk Euclid taught them to make great walls and ditches to keep back the water, and by Geometry he measured the land and parcelled it out into sections and caused every man to enclose his own portion with walls and ditches and thus it became a country abounding in all kinds of produce, and of young people and of men and women : so that the youthful population increased so much as to render earning a livelihood difficult. And the lords of the country drew together and took counsel how they might help their children who had no competent livelihood in order to provide for themselves and their children, for they had so many. And at the council amongst them was this worthy Clerk Euclid and when he saw that all of them could devise no remedy in the matter be said to them "Lay your orders upon your sons and I will teach them a science by which they may live as gentlemen, under the condition that they shall be sworn to me to uphold the regulations that I shall lay upon them." And both they and the king of the country and all the lords agreed thereto with one consent.

It is but reasonable that every man should agree to that which tended to profit himself ; and so they took their sons to Euclid to be ruled by him and he taught them the Craft of Masonry and gave it the name of Geometry on account of the parcelling out of the ground which he had taught the people at the time of making the walls and ditches, as aforesaid, to keep out the water. And Isodoris says in Ethomologies that Euclid called the craft Geometry.

And there this worthy clerk Euclid gave it a name and taught it to the lord's sons of that land whom he had as pupils.

And he gave them a charge. That they should call each other Fellow and no otherwise, they being all of one craft and of the same gentle birth, lords' sons. And also that the most skilful should be governor of the work and should be called master ; and other charges besides, which are written in the Book of Charges. And so they worked for the lords of the land and built cities and towns, castles and temples and lords' palaces.

During the time that the children of Israel dwelt in Egypt they learned the craft of Masonry. And after they were driven out of Egypt they came into the promised land, which is now called Jerusalem, and they occupied that land and the charges were observed there. And [at] the making of Solomon's Temple which king David began, King David loved masons well, and gave them [wages] nearly as they are now. And at the making of the Temple in Solomon's time, as stated in the Bible in the third book of Kings and the fifth chapter, Solomon held four score thousand masons at work. And the son of the king of Tyre was his master mason. And in other chronicles and in old books of masonry, it is said that Solomon confirmed the charges that David his father had given to masons. And Solomon himself taught them their usages differing but slightly from the customs now in use.

And from thence this worthy science was brought into France and into many other regions.

At one time there was a worthy king in France called Carolus Secondus, that is to say Charles the Second. And this Charles was elected king of France by the grace of God and also by right of descent. And some men say he was elected by good fortune, which is false as by the chronicles he was of the blood royal. And this same king Charles was a mason before he became king. And after he was king he loved masons and cherished them and gave them charges and usages of his devising, of which some are yet in force in France ; and he ordained that they should have an assembly once a year and come and speak together in order that the masters and follows might regulate all things amiss.

And soon after that came St. Adhabelle into England and he converted St. Alban to Christianity. And St. Alban loved well masons and he was the first to give them charges and customs in England, And he ordained [wages] adequate to pay for their toil.

And after that there was a worthy king in England, called Athelstan, and his youngest son loved well the science of Geometry ; and he knew well, as well as the masons themselves, that their handicraft was the practice of the science of Geometry. Therefore he drew to their councils (or took counsel, or lessons, of them) and learned the practical part of that science in addition to his theoretical (or book) knowledge. For of the speculative part he was a master. And he loved well masonry and masons. And he became a mason himself. And he give them charges and usages such as are now customary in England and in other countries. And he ordained that they should have reasonable pay. And he purchased a free patent of the king that they might hold an assembly at what time they thought reasonable and come together to consult. Of the which charges, usages and assembly it is written and taught in our Book of Charges; wherefore I leave it for the present.

Good men! for this cause and in this way Masonry first arose. It befell, once upon a time, that great lords had so many free begotten children that their possessions were not extensive enough to provide for their future. Therefore they took counsel how to provide for their children and find them all honest livelihood. And they sent for wise masters of the worthy science of Geometry, that through their wisdom they might provide them with some honest living. Then one of them that was called Euclid a most subtil and wise inventor regulated [that science] and art and called it Masonry. And so in this art of his he honestly taught the children of great lords according to the desire of the fathers and the free consent of their children. And having taught them with great care for a certain time they were not all alike capable of exercising the said art, wherefore the said master Euclid ordained that those that surpassed the others in skill should be honoured above the others. And [comman]ded to call the more skilful "master" and for [him] to instruct the less skilful. The which masters were called masters of nobility, of knowledge and skill in that art. Nevertheless they commanded that they that were of less knowledge should not be called servants or subjects, but fellows, on account of the nobility of their gentle blood. In this manner was the aforesaid art begun in the land of Egypt by the aforesaid master Euclid and so it spread from country to country and from kingdom to kingdom

Many years after, in the time of king Athelstan, sometime king of England, by common assent of his Council and other great lords of the land on account of great defects found amongst masons, a certain rule was ordained for them.

Once a year or every three years as might appear needful to the king and great lords of the land and all the comunity, congregations should be called by the masters from country to country and from province to province of all masters, masons and fellows in the said art. And at such congregations those that are made masters shall be examined in the articles hereafter written and be ransacked whether they be able and skilful in order to serve the lords to their profit and to the honour of the aforesaid art. And moreover they shall be charged to well and truly expend the goods of their lords, as well of the lowest as of the highest ; for those are their lords for the time being of whom they take their pay in recompense of their service and toil.

The first article is this. That every master of this art should be wise, and true to the lord who employs him, expending his goods carefully as he would his own were expended; and not give more pay to any mason than he knows him to have earned, according to the dearth (or scarcity and therefore price) of corn and victuals in the country and this without favouritism, for every man is to be rewarded according to his work.

The Second article is this. That every master of the art shall be warned beforehand to come to his congregation in order that he may duly come, there, unless he may [be] excused for some cause or other. But if he be found [i.e., accused of being] rebellious at such congregation, or at fault in any way to his employer's harm or the reproach of this art, he shall not be excused unless he be in peril of death. And though he be in peril of death, yet must, he give notice of his illness, to the master who is the president of the gathering.

The [third] article is this. That no master take no apprentice for a shorter term than seven years at least, for the reason that such as have been bound a shorter time cannot adequately learn their art, nor be able to truly serve their employer and earn the pay that a mason should.

The fourth article is this. That no master shall for any reward take as an apprentice a bondsman born, because his lord to whom he is a bondsman might take him, as he is entitled to, from his art and carry him away with him from out the Lodge, or out of the place he is in. And because his fellows peradventure might help him and take his part, and thence manslaughter might arise ; therefore it is forbidden.

And there is another reason; because his art was begun by the freely begotten children of great lords, as aforesaid.

The fifth article is this. That no master shall pay more to his apprentice during the time of his apprenticeship, whatever profit he may take thereby, than he well knows him to have deserved of the lord that employs him; and not even quite so much, in order that the lord of the works where he is taught may have some profit by his being taught there.

The sixth article is this. That no master from covetousness or for gain shall accept an apprentice that is unprofitable; that is, having any maim (or defect) by reason of which he is incapable of doing a mason's proper work.

The seventh article is this. That no master shall knowingly help or cause to be maintained and sustained any common nightwalker robber by which nightwalking they may be rendered incapable of doing a fair day's work and toil: a condition of things by which their fellows might be made wrath.

The eighth article is this. Should it befall that a perfect and skilful mason come and apply for work and find one working who is incompetent and unskilful, the master of the place shall discharge the incompetent and engage the skilful one, to the advantage of the employer.

The ninth article is this. That no master shall supplant another. For it is said in the art of masonry that no man can so well complete a work to the advantage of the lord, begun by another as he who began it intending to end it in accordance with his own plans, or [he] to whom he shows his plans.

These regulation following were made by the lords (employers) and masters of divers provinces and divers congregations of masonry.

[First point] To wit : whosoever desires to become a mason, it behoves him before all things to [love] God and the holy Church and all the Saints ; and his master and follows as his own brothers.

The second point. He must give a fair day's work for his pay.

The third [point]. He shall hele the counsel or his fellows in lodge and in chamber, and wherever masons meet.

The fourth point. He shall be no traitor to the art and do it no harm nor conform to any enactments against the art nor against the members thereof : but he shall maintain it in all honour to the best of his ability.

The fifth point. When he receives his pay he shall take it without murmuring, as may be arranged at the time by the master; and he shall fulfil the agreement regarding the hours of work and rest, as ordained and set by the master.

The sixth point. In case of disagreement between him and his fellows, he shall unquestioningly obey the master and be silent thereon at the bidding of his master, or of his master's warden in his master's absence, until the next following holiday and shall then settle the matter according to the verdict of his fellows; and not upon a work-day because of the hindrance to the work and to the lord's interests.

The seventh point. He shall not covet the wife nor the daughter of his master or of his fellows unless it be in marriage neither shall he hold concubines, on account of the discord this might create amongst them.

The eighth point. Should it befall him to be his master's warden, he shall be a true mediator between his master and his fellows : and he shall be active in his master's absence to the honour of his master and the profit of the lord who employs him.

The ninth point. If he be more wise and skilful than his fellow working with him in the Lodge or in any other place, and he perceive that for want of skill, he is about to spoil the stone upon which he is working and can teach him to improve the stone, he shall instruct and help him ; so that love may increase the more amongst them and the work of his employer be not lost.

When the master and fellows, being forewarned are come to such congregations, the sheriff of the country or the mayor of the city or alderman of the town in which the congregation is held, shall if need be, be fellow and associate of the master of the congregation, to help him against disobedient members to maintain the rights of the realm.

And at the commencement of the proceedings, new men who have never been charged before are to be charged in this manner. Ye shall never be thieves nor thieves' maintainers, and shall do a fair day's work and toil for your pay that you take of the lord, and shall render true accounts to your fellows in all matters which should be accounted for to them, and love them as yourselves. And ye shall be true to the king of England and to the realm : and that ye keep with all your might and [power] all the aforesaid articles.

After that an enquiry shall be held whether any master or fellow summoned to the meeting, have broken any of the beforesaid articles, which, if they have done, it shall be then and there adjudicated upon.

Therefore be it known; if any master or fellow being forewarned to come to the congregation, be contumacious and appear not; or having trespassed against any of the aforesaid articles shall be convicted ; he shall forswear his masonry and shall no longer exercise the craft. And if he presume so to do, the sheriff of the country in which he may be found at work shall put him in prison and take all his goods for the use of the king, until his (the king's) grace be granted and showed him.

For this cause chiefly were these congregations ordained ; that the lowest as well as the highest might be well and truly served in the aforesaid art throughout all the kingdom of England.

Amen, so mote it be.

The Torgau Ordinances
*Concerning the worshipful Masters of Stonemasons
of the Craft, the Wardens,
and the Fellows of the Craft.*
circa 1462

All Articles and Statutes as they are written in the Book; how each and every one in his conduct and station in the craft shall demean himself, both here in Zwickau and elsewhere in all lands; as in the Book, so stands hereafter written, each article separately.

In the name of the Father, and of the Son, and of the Holy Ghost, in the name of the blessed Virgin Mary, and in honour of the four crowned martyrs, we workmasters of the stonemasons make known: To all princes and lords, cities and burgers, and also peasants, of whatsoever rank they be, of the Church or of the world, that the several workmasters in the Oberland have assembled on two days at Regenspurgk and at Strasburgk, and have beheld such great evil and disorders in the work, and failings done in all lands of master, wardens, and fellows, therefore have they carefully sent into this land a book of the Ordinances and rules, and do exhort us therein, by the holy oath which we have sworn unto masonry, to accept and confirm these Ordinances in this land according to usage, as this Book clearly points out. This have we done, workmasters in all these lands of Meydeburgk arid Halberstat, Hildeszlieim and Mullburgk and Merseburgk, and at Meihssen, Voitlandt, Duringen, HartzIandt, the majority of us being present together, or our wardens on our part having full power, on the two days of St Bartholomew and St Michael at Torgau; as is usually written, after the birth of our dear Lord Christ, and in the one thousand four hundred and sixty-second year, have we confirmed the regulations of the Book and the contents thereof, and are at one therewith, and thereto have sworn by the saints.

These Articles are to be maintained in all lands, far and wide, be they of the Church or of the world, and we have enjoined upon all judges and overmasters to rule by such and to hold it in high esteem according to the usages and necessities of the land, and to keep watch over all that concerns masonry and buildings, and concerns not states nor cities; and to adjudge penalties in all matters relating to masonry; and it shall be done with consent of the lords who are the inheritors of the land, and to help the right. Therefore have we drawn up divers articles from the Book for the general good, and the Book shall remain in high honour in such places as we shall deposit it every year; and there will we hear once a year if any offence have been committed against master builders or fellows, that such be adjudged and atoned, and also if the lords of states, be they spiritual or temporal, have any cause of complaint as regards their buildings; and they shall submit them to such craftsmen as are chosen to be chief masters [literally Overmaster] in writing or by speech, and they shall be heard according to builders' usage. Therefore shall the overmasters that are there, and have taken the oath and have summoned them on the yearly day, whenever it be, give them hearing as is customary, for the sake of the building; and if the lords suffer any loss, make good such loss according to the judgment of the masters; but if he come not and answer not for himself, so shall he be proscribed and lay down all rule over his fellows, and none shall esteem or hold him true, nor shall he be true man.

And we before-mentioned masters, wardens, and fellows have taken and drawn up from the Book for brevity, divers Ordinances that are obligatory on all workmasters in authority and fellows; that the real Book remain intact, and be only read there when we hold our yearly assembly.

And when the lords will not have it so, then shall it not be so; and what the lords will not have, that shall be left undone of all such articles as are not of necessity and the masters in such lands are not bound to enforce, according to their oath, such articles as contents of the Book of the craft; to declare what shall be done for the service of God, and also for sustenance, this is not of necessity to write now; every master knows this well who has formerly heard it,

And all these articles have been drawn up from the letter of the ancient lodge rights, that were instituted by the holy worthy crowned martyrs, by name Claudius, and Christorius, and Significamus, to the honour and praise of the Holy Trinity and Mary the Queen of Heaven.

1. Therefore have we made divers rules and statutes with the help of God.

And every master shall on all acknowledged fasts cause four masses to be said.

And on St Peter's Day, when he was raised at Antioch, shall he also cause four masses to be said.

And the first mass of the Holy Trinity, the other of our dear Lady, the third of the four crowned martyrs, the fourth for all who have died in the guild, and for all who help our craft and labour therein.

2. And the other masters shall also cause four masses to be said every feast of our Lady, one for each of the aforesaid souls, and the money wherewith he pays for the mass, the same money shall he take from the box, and the remainder shall he give to the craft box.

And for God's service shall every master of a work, be it great or small, give on each fast of our Lady one old groat.

And every fellow shall give every week to the box one penny for God's service.

3. And furthermore, no master shall undertake a work unless he have proved himself such to the craft, that the craftsmen be protected.

4. And should there appear a master that has not previously worked as master, then shall he have twain proven masters to speak for him, that he may be placed at the head of the work, and thus shall he be accepted.

5. And where it is intended to raise new and stately buildings, then shall the lords of the work choose them a master whomsoever they will, and are enjoined to take two or four workmasters, and shall inquire of them on their oath which they have sworn to the guild whether the master be truly able to undertake the work.

6. For, if lords or cities appoint one who has not formerly undertaken such work, for stately buildings and take not craftsmen, and loss occur thereby, thereof shall nor master nor fellows judge, neither punish.

7. And no master shall undertake a work unless he be able to accomplish it; and should it be that he fail herein, it is for the lords of the work to restrain him, and also for us craftsmen. And that must he

rue with one and twenty pounds of wax, and to the lord must he make good the loss.

8. And every one shall keep his time according to the ancient traditionary usages of the land; if he do that he is free, and even if he do it not with counsel, according to the usages of the land and the craft.

9. And no master shall diminish or reduce the pay.

10. And every master shall be upright in all things. He shall incite neither warden nor fellow nor apprentice to evil, nor to aught whence harm may arise.

11. And every master shall keep his lodge free of all strife, yea, his lodge shall he keep pure as the seat of justice.

12. And no master shall bear false witness in his lodge, neither shall he defile it in any manner.

13. Therefore shall no master allow a harlot to enter his lodge, but if any one have aught to commune with her he shall depart from the place of labour so far as one may cast a gavel.

14. If other masters learn thereof, they shall fine him for each offence in five pounds of wax.

15. Nevertheless, it is not for the fellows to fine any master, but they are to withdraw from him and forbid other craftsmen his lodge, so that none consort with him, until he shall have been fined.

16. Whatsoever master shall rob any place, or take aught from any place of labour whereby any one suffer loss, or if he be murderer or outlaw, him shall ye altogether thrust from out the guild of the craft and suffer him in naught.

17. Whatsoever master shall summon another master before the law, or suffer him to be so done by, or do him evil or speak ill of him, he is empty of all honour, and fit for neither fellow nor master.

18. A master shall appoint his warden, master and warden being both present; and he shall appoint no warden unless he be able thereto, so that the craftsmen and he be supplied. He shall impress him with the wardenship, and receive his oath to the saints on square and gauge to prevent harm to the building or the master.

19. So shall neither master nor his wardens be illegally set over the fellows.

20. When a master has set a warden, the fellows shall swear to be obedient unto him as unto the master, and the warden shall pledge master and fellows.

21. And no master shall accept any fee from a warden or fellow on account of his requirements, nor any offering; for if he be not able to earn his wages then shall he be discharged on the Saturday.

22. No master shall out of goodwill accept any apprentice before he have served his time and won his right; that is not in the master's power to the extent of one week.

23. And the master shall appoint each week a treasurer, who shall make all payments, and account each week to the new treasurer, and shall be answerable to him [the master] for the contents of the box.

24. And the master has power, if he so will, to rest in the lodge at vesper tide.

25. And if a master or fellow come free of the craft or trade, and demand a mark of a workmaster, to him shall he grant his wish, and he shall give for the service of God that which shall be adjudged of master and fellows. And to master and fellows shall he pledge the mark doubly.

26. No master shall withhold his mark from his apprentice for a further space than xiii, days, unless it be that the apprentice has wasted his master's time, he shall then first do his behest before that and the feast.

27. And no master shall show any reluctance to pledge his apprentice's mark, and the several clericals whom he may bid thereto, with a penny wheaten bread of xv. gr., a loaf of xv. gr., meat, and two stoups of wine; and the apprentice shall not bid more than x fellows, and if he bid more then shall he buy more, that the master suffer not thereby.

28. The master shall knock with three blows, the warden with two consecutively, and one for announcements at morning, noon, and eve, as is the old usage of the land.

29. The master may appoint an apprentice who serves for knowledge to the office of warden, if he be able to maintain it, in order that the building suffer not,

The Torgau Ordinances

30. The master may lend his apprentice a mark to travel during his apprenticeship, if the master have no employment, and must let him travel.

31. No master shall allow his apprentice to pledge his mark, unless he have served his time.

32. No master shall lay snares for another and entice away his apprentice, so reads the letter.

33. No master shall employ any one who has brought himself to shame or dishonour either by word or deed; he is worse than a hound; him shall the master set down as void of honour, likewise also the fellows.

34. And no master or warden shall be held of good report who borrows and remains owing and is unwilling to pay. If this be brought home to him, he shall be warned and told to make it good by a certain time, and if he do this not, and do it not with the approval of him to whom he is indebted, then shall he be debarred from all employment until he comply with the wish of his creditor.

35. Also no master shall defraud or beslander the other, nor compete for his work unless it be that he have deserted it, or given it up, or permitted or prayed him so to do; so may he do it without fear. But should he do as aforesaid, the other masters shall cast him out.

36. Shame or dishonour one master the other by word or deed, and bring it not home to him, he shall be cast from out the craft.

37. Whatsoever master shall slight another's work, and is himself not able thereto, him shall ye proscribe.

38. And no master shall employ any fellow who has slandered another or doeth evil, and consorts with public women, and who in the hostelries or houses where they work, speaketh unchastely with maids or matrons, or is incontinent therein, who goeth not to confession or doeth that which is wrong; he shall be proscribed and held an evil-doer.

39. And a master may hold a general court. in his lodge over his own fellows, and he shall judge righteously by his oath, and not of hatred, or of friendship, or of enmity.

40. And furthermore, no master shall judge alone of that which touches honour or good repute; but there shall be together three masters who shall then judge such matters.

41. And farther, every master shall inquire of his fellows every quarter, on their oath, if any hatred or envy be amongst them that might disadvantage the building; such shall he judge and put aside, and whatsoever fellow fail to comply herein, him shall he discharge, that no strife be found amongst them; and even though it please not the lords or the master builder, yet shall the master do right and avoid wrong, that he may keep his oath.

42. And he shall every quarter-day hold a hearing of lords and craftsmen, whether any offence were, whether they have wasted their time, lived riotously, gamed or otherwise acted disorderly, whence harm might come to wardens or master, that shall they make known to the master that he may punish therefore as is meet; and if the lords declare it not to the master and forgive it the fellows, then shall the master not punish on account thereof; and if a lord of the building know thereof and the master punish not, then doth he not fulfill his oath.

43. Is aught to be judged amongst masters concerning good report, or which might drive away work, or cause a false state of affairs, whence injury might arise, concerning year work, or large buildings, that shall be judged where the Book of the Ordinances is deposited, and the masters assemble every year on the day as is aforesaid; then shall the masters elect them an over-judge, and the wardens and fellows shall elect Sheriffs to the judge, and they shall judge by plaint and answer on the oath as administered; and if they in anything disagree, they shall take to themselves arbiters, and take counsel together that justice be done to all men.

44. And masters and fellows shall punish each other amongst themselves, righteously for the best, that the lords may not interfere through their perjury.

45. Should the masters have one amongst them, be he master or fellow, and will not be in obedience, and set himself up against these ordinances, we pray all lords that none take his part or defend him on his petition; should he nevertheless, against all usage, be defended against us, we know well, according to the Ordinances, how we shall then demean ourselves.

46. Should there be a master or fellow who would defend himself contrary to usage, ye are to call upon all cities and lords, and lay the matter before them, and enjoin them to help us maintain our right;

The Torgau Ordinances

for to him who shall help us to our right will we also be obedient when they require our services.

47. And thus shall be the wardens, and maintain thus the old traditionary lodge rights, according to ancient usage and the Book, and the Ordinances of the oath.

48. Every warden shall preserve his lodge, and all that he has sworn to, and all that is entrusted to him of the place of work, that shall he keep and maintain for the good of the building.

49. The warden shall show goodwill to the fellows, and show them, without anger and

of go goodwill, what they shall ask of him. He shall use no more than right with any fellow or apprentice, he shall always prove level and plumb-rule, and all that pertains thereto, that -no, faults be therein, and if the master himself prove not or prepare suck then is it the warden's part; and should the master at any time learn thereof that he have neglected these articles, he thereby incurs a penalty of xij. kr. to the master.

50. The warden shall willingly choose and mark out stones for the fellows and apprentices, and inspect and see that they be well and truly made of the fellows; and if he do not so, and the master discover errors that anything be untrue, then shall he forfeit to the master viij. kr. and the fellow vj. kr.

51. And if a warden mark a stone because it is of no use, then shall he [the workman] lose his wages that he had otherwise earned on that stone, unless it be made of use.

52. Whatsoever warden shall levy a fine on account of negligence, or other offence, and shall not acknowledge and announce the same, he shall forfeit twice the fine that has been incurred.

63. No warden shall deprive his master of his building by word or deed; he shall not injure him behind his back with false words; as oft as he so does, shall he be declared worthless and of bad report, and shall no master, neither the fellows, suffer him, but whosoever shall stand by him shall like him be worthless.

54. A warden shall knock at the right time, and shall delay it on no one's account

55. Is a master not on the works, or absent therefrom, then has the warden full power to do or leave undone that which is right in the masters absence.

56. And the warden shall mark the under side of the stones of fellows and apprentices, should the fellows and apprentices fail to answer the knocks, and not appear to the right time at breakfast; and if he take not the fines so shall he pay them himself.

57. The warden shall not quarrel himself, or incite any thereto, either at meals or at work; he shall always comport himself right amicably and justly; he shall keep the fellows to their stones or work, be it what it may, that no harm may ensue to buildings or masters; and the master shall decide the fine, according to the loss he suffers thereby.

58. And no warden shall allow meals in the lodge during working hours, but only at the vesper rest.

59. Nor shall he suffer that more be spent at the vesper meal, but only one penny, unless there be a pledge feast, or that a travelling fellow be arrived; then is the warden empowered to cease work one hour earlier.

60. A warden has power to further a travelling fellow to the nearest work, also power to discharge on the pay-evening, even if he be not a builder or master.

61. He has power to allow every fellow or apprentice a reasonable time without loss.

62. And every warden shall be the first in the lodge of a morning, and after dinner at the opening; and the last to leave, be it at noon or at eventide, that all fellows may follow his example, and come to labour all the sooner. Should he fail herein, and the master come to hear thereof, whatsoever loss is thereby incurred, such loss shall the warden pay.

63. The warden shall help preserve all privileges of the lodges and places of labour.

64. And the warden shall make no overcharge on workshop fines, but according to the traditionary usages of the pay shall he levy them; and if he do otherwise, so. is he unworthy.

65. And he shall maintain all things appertaining to the place of labour, and keep them to use, even as the master.

Of the Ordinances of the Fellows, how they shall comport themselves.

66. Whatsoever fellow shall offer his services to another master before he shall have taken his discharge from the master with whom he serves, such fellow shall forfeit one pound of wax and be discharged.

67. Whatsoever fellow shall carry tales or create scandal between the master or other craftsmen, he shall. forfeit one-half his week's wages.

68. Whoever takes another's tools without leave shall forfeit ij. kr.

69. Whatsoever fellow shall falsely apply his templet, or put it by before he have proved his work, and that without leave or before the master or warden shall have inspected his work, or shall leave his square hanging on the stone, or allow the level to lie about and not hang it up though it be furnished with a hole thereto, or lets his stone fall from the bench, or forces the pick iron from off the handle, or leaves his gauge otherwise than in the place appointed therefor, or closes not the window near his bench, — whoever shall do anything of the aforementioned articles, he shall forfeit iij. kr. for every such offence.

70. Whatsoever fellow shall speak the other ill, or call him liar in ill-will or earnest, or is foul-mouthed in the place of labour, he shall pay xij. kr. to forfeit.

71. Whatsoever fellow shall laugh another to scorn, or jeer at him, or call him by a nickname, he shall pay 15 kr. to forfeit.

72. Whatsoever fellow shall not offer assistance to turn his stone this way or that, to fetch it or to turn it over when necessary, or places his mark thereon as if it were truly made, and that before it shall have been proven, so that it be passed unproven to the store, or improperly finishes his work, he shall stand to forfeit one half pound of wax.

73. Whatsoever fellow shall drink or eat to excess, so that it become known, he shall forfeit one weeks wages and j. pound of wax.

74. Whatsoever fellow shall use force in places of labour or of refreshment, or shall consort with or treat notorious females in the presence of godly women, he shall be discharged, and the weeks pay that he has earned that same week shall be retained and given to the box.

75. Whatsoever fellow shall squander lodge moneys, or pilfer, or murder, or steal, or commit any other crime, or disports himself in the land with ungodly women, and goeth not to confession and doeth not God's will, he shall be cast out from the craft and proscribed for ever.

76. Whosoever shall slander another and spread evil report of him, and justifieth it not, he shall make atonement to the satisfaction of masters and fellows.

77. Who shall accuse another and bring it not home to him, him shall ye severely punish, that he be careful of his speech another time; but if he prove it to the satisfaction of the fellows, according as the offence is shall ye judge, and no fellow shall ye judge out of malice.

78. And no fellow shall lord it over an apprentice, but he shall lay his plaint before the master, wherein the apprentice have offended him, and he shall punish him therefore.

79. And no warden, nor fellow, nor apprentice shall be his own judge, for if they do that, which of right belongs to the master, then are they deserving of a fine; and the master shall be judge and none other.

80. And the fellows shall not fine each other without the knowledge of masters and wardens.

81. And no fellow shall hew stones with a proscribed fellow, unless it be that he have made amends on that day of the year, when the masters do assemble.

82. And no fellow shall lead a woman of evil report into the lodges or places of labour, neither shall he take her where masters are together; who so doeth shall pay iiij. pounds of wax.

83. Whatsoever fellow shall make unto himself holy days in the week when he should be at labour, they are not holy, and he shall not be instructed.

84. And whatsoever fellow is absent when he should be at work, even after the breakfast is eaten, he shall not be paid for his time till noon; and if he remain absent all day and come to supper, then shall he not be paid for the whole day.

85. Whatsoever fellow shall not, for his master's honour, accompany him to church on Sundays and the greater fasts at high mass, but remains without, and without leave, he shall pay iiij. kr. to God's service.

86. Whatsoever warden or fellow be not with his master at the stroke of one on the Monday afternoon, and keep with him the vesper rest, and hear what he shall do on that Monday, he shall pay the supper bill; if he set himself up against this he shall be discharged that Monday for disobedience, but if he pray excuse at his entrance, so shall he pay nothing and is free.

87. And every master may discharge a fellow from the building without causing anger, if it seem right to him.

88. And every fellow may take his discharge any pay evening if it please him, for none is bound to the other.

89. Whatsoever fellow takes service of a master for the winter ' he shall be with him till St John's Day, when the crown is hung up; unless it be that the fellow have aught serious against the master, whereby the work may sustain injury, then may he justly leave him. And if the fellow know aught to the master's dishonour, and keep silent, and hold his peace winter and summer, and denies it, that fellow keepeth not good faith, and is meet for no fellow.

90. And no fellow shall give master or warden any offering for the sake of work; with him shall no fellow work until he have been fined.

91. And no fellow shall do another's work for money, but he shall do one piece for another, or do it for him to his honour.

92. No fellow shall speak against either warden or master.

93. And no fellow shall carry about with him any knife or other weapon other than one knife of half an ell in length, be it at work or refreshment; if it be longer, then shall he pay vij. kr. as fine, and also lay it aside.

94. If a fellow have not served his time, or have bought his mark and not honestly earned it, or if a hired servant or help establishes himself and teaches to work in stone, with him shall no man take service.

95. And no fellow shall speak M of his master or warden unless he wish to make it known to those who stand in that master's service.

96. And no fellow shall fleece or maltreat the master builders, but they shall willingly do as the in builders instruct them if the master or warden be not on the works; but if they be there, so shall they tell the master or warden what is necessary to be said.

97. And no fellow shall complain of another fellow to the master builder, but to the workmaster.

98. And no master builder shall correct any strife amongst the fellows unless he be desired to do so of the master.

99. And no fellow shall take service with those who employ a master builder without the master's consent.

100. Whatsoever fellow shall be treated by the master builder, with him shall no fellow consort.

101. Whatsoever offence the master builder commit, either against warden or fellow, that shall they lay before the master, and have strife with none.

102. And no warden or fellow shall secretly take pay without the master's knowledge, and though the master builder should wish to punish, it is for the master only to decide how he will arrange with his fellows.

103. And no fellow shall go with another to the closet, but one after the other, that the place of labour stand not empty; or one shall bear the other into the lodge, or pay ij. kr.

104. And no fellow shall do aught, or take stone for aught, or go out from the lodge, without the master's leave; and the master shall decide what he shall pay.

105. And when a fellow travels, then when he comes to a new lodge shall he leave his master in friendship, and not in anger.

106. And if a travelling fellow come before work is knocked off, he shall earn his day's wages. And every travelling fellow, when he has received the donation, shall go from one to the other and shall thank him therefore.

107. And this is the greeting wherewith every fellow shall greet; when he first goeth into the lodge, thus shall he say:

"God greet ye, God guide ye, God reward ye, ye honourable overmaster, warden, and trusty fellows;" and the master or warden shall thank him, that he may know who is the superior in the lodge.

Then shall the fellow address himself to the same, and say: "The master" (naming him) "bids me greet you worthily;" and he shall go to the fellows from one to the other and greet each in a friendly manner, even as he greeted the superior.

And then shall they all, master, and wardens, and fellows, pledge him as is the custom, and m is already written of the greeting and pledge; but not to him whom they hold for no true man, he shall be fined one pound of wax, xxiiij. kr.

108. And every fellow when he returns thanks, if he wish for employment, shall ask of the master, and the master shall employ him till the next pay day, and deny him not, that the fellow may cam his living; and should the master have no more work than he can perform alone, the master shall help him find work.

109. And every travelling fellow shall ask first for a pick, thereafter for a piece of stone, and furthermore for tools, and that shall be lent to him of goodwill.

110. And every fellow shall pray the other fellows, and they shall not turn a deaf car; they shall all help; "help me that God may help ye;" and when they have helped him he shall doff his hat, and shall say, God thank the master, and warden, and worthy fellows."

111. And if any fellow be in need on account of sickness. and have not wherewithal to live because he lieth sick he shall be assisted from the box and if he recover he shall pay it.

112. And if any fellow shall make a journey for the guild in that that concerns the craft his expenses also shall be paid him out of the box.

The Strasburg Manuscript
circa 1464

The Constitutions of Strasburg

In the name of the Father, and of the Son, and of the Holy Ghost, and of our gracious Mother Mary, and also of her blessed servants, the holy four crowned martyrs of everlasting memory: considering that true friendship, unanimity, and obedience are the foundation of all good; therefore, and for the general advantage and free will of all princes, nobles, lords, cities, chapters, and convents, who may desire at this time or in future to build churches, choirs, or other great works of stone, and edifices; that they may be the better provided and supplied, and also for the benefit and requirements of the masters and fellows of the whole craft of Masonry, and masons in Germany, and more especially to avoid in future, between those of the craft, dissensions, differences, costs, and damages, by which irregular acts many masters have suffered grievously, contrary to the good customs and ancient usages maintained and practiced in good faith by the seniors and patrons of the craft in ancient times. But that we may continue to abide therein in a true and peaceful way, have we, masters and fellows all, of the said craft, congregated in chapters at Spries, at Strasburg, set or not, then shall such master not pull down the set stones, nor in and at Regensburg, in the name and on behalf of ourselves and of all other masters and fellows of our whole common craft above mentioned, renewed and revised these ancient usages, and kindly and affably agreed upon these statues and fraternity; and having by common consent drawn up the same, have also vowed and promised, for ourselves and all our successors, to keep them faithfully, as hereafter stands writ:

a. Firstly: If any of the articles in these statues should prove to be too strict and severe, or others too light and mild, then may those who are of the fraternity, by a majority, modify decrease, or increase such articles, according to the requirements of the time, or country, or circumstance. The resolutions of those who shall meet together in chapters after the manner of this book shall thenceforth be observed, in accordance with the oath taken by every one.'

b. Item: Whoever of his own free will desires to enter into this fraternity, according to the regulation as hereafter stands writ in this book, shall promise to keep all the points and articles, for then only can he be of our craft. Those shall be masters, who can design and erect such costly edifices and works, for the execution of which they are authorized and privileged, and shall not work with any other craft, unless they choose so to do. Masters as well as fellows must conduct themselves honorably, and not infringe upon the rights of others, or they may be punished, according to these statues, on the occasion of every such transgression.

c. Item: Whatever regular works and buildings are now in progress of erection by journey work- namely, Strasburg, Cologne, Vienna, and Passau, and other such works, and also in the Lodges which belong to them, and, according to custom, have been hitherto finished by journey work, such buildings and works as before mentioned shall be continued by journey work, and in no wise by task work; so that nothing be cut short of the work, to the damage of the contract as far as possible.

d. Item: If any craftsman who has had regular work should die, then any craftsman or master, skilled in Masonry, and sufficient and able for work, may aspire to complete said work, so that the lords owning or superintending such building may again be supplied with the requirements of Masonry. So also may any fellow who understands such Masonry.

e. Item: Any master may, in addition to his own work, undertake a work abroad, or a master who has no such work may likewise undertake it, in which case he may give such work or building in good faith, in journey work, and continue it as best he can or may, so that the work and progress be not interrupted, according to the regulations and customs of Masonry. If a master fails to satisfy those persons who committed the work to him, and reliable information be given thereof, then shall the said master be called to account by the craft, corrected, and punished, after having been sentenced; but if the lords are not willing so to do, then may he do it as they choose, be it by task or journey work.

f. Item: If any master, who has had such a work or building, die, and another master comes and finds such stone-work, be the stone work any wise cast away the hewn and unset stones, without previous counsel and agreement with other craftsmen, so that the owners and other honorable persons, who caused such edifice to be builded, be not put to unjust expense, and that also the master who left such work not be defamed. But if the owners choose to have such work removed, then he may have it done, provided he seeks no undue advantage thereby.

g. Item: Neither shall the master, not those who have undertaken such work, hire out anything that relates to or concerns hewn stones and what belongs to them, be it stone, lime, or sand; but to break or hew by contract or by journey work he may be allowed without risk.

h. Item: If masons be required for hewing or setting stone, the master may set such at work, if they are able, so that the lords be not hindered, and those who are thus employed shall not be subject to these regulations unless of their own free will.

i. Item: Two masters shall not share in the same work or building, unless it be a small one, which can be finished in the course of a year. Such a work he may have in common with him that is a brother.

k. Item: If any master accepts a work in contract and makes a design for the same, how it shall be builded, then he shall not cut anything short of the design, but shall execute it according to the plan which he has shown to the lords, cities, or people, so that nothing be altered.:

l. Any master or fellow who shall take away from another master of the fraternity of craftsmen a work on which he is engaged, or who shall endeavor to disposes him of such work, clandestinely or openly, without the knowledge or consent of the master who has such work, be the same small or great, he shall be called to account. No master or fellow shall keep fellowship with him, nor shall any fellow of the fraternity work for him, so long as he is engaged in the work which he has thus dishonestly acquired, nor until he has asked pardon, and given satisfaction to him whom he has driven from his work, and shall also have been punished in the fraternity by the masters, as is ordained by these statutes.

m. Item: If any one accepts in whole or in part any work which he does not understand how to execute, not having consulted any craftsman thereon, nor having applied to the Lodge, he shall in no wise undertake the work; but if he attempts to do so, then shall no fellow take work with him, so that the lords be not put to expense by such ignorant master.

n. Item: No workman, nor master, nor Parlirer, nor fellowcraft, shall instruct any one, whosoever, who is not of our craft, in any part, if he has not in his day practiced Masonry.

o. Item: No craftsman nor master shall take money from a fellow for teaching or instructing him in anything belonging to Masonry, nor shall any parlirer or fellowcraft instruct any one for money's sake; but if one wishes to instruct the other, they may do so mutually or for fraternal affection.

p. Item: A master who has a work or a building for himself may have three apprentices, and may also set to work fellows of the same Lodge- that is, if his lords so permit; but if he have more buildings than one, then shall he have no more than two apprentices on the afore-mentioned building, so that he shall not have more than five apprentices on all his buildings.

No craftsman or master shall be received in the fraternity who goes not yearly to the Holy Communion or who keep not Christian discipline, or who squanders his substance at play; but should any one be inadvertently accepted into the fraternity who does these things as aforesaid, then shall no master nor fellow keep fellowship with him until he desists therefrom, and has been punished therefor by those of the fraternity.

No craftsman nor master shall live in adultery while engaged in Masonry; but if such a one will not desist therefrom, then shall no traveling fellow nor mason work in company with him, nor keep fellowship with him.

q. Item: If a fellowcraft takes work with a master who is not accepted into the fraternity of craftsmen, then shall the said fellow not be punishable therefor. So also, if a fellow take work with a city master, or with another master, and be there set to work, that may he well do, so that every fellow may find work; but nevertheless such fellow shall keep the regulations as hereinbefore and hereinafter written, and shall also contribute his fee to the fraternity, although he be not employed in the Lodges of the fraternity, or with his fellow brethren.

But if a fellow would take unto himself a lawful wife, and not being employed in a Lodge, would establish himself in a city, and be obliged to serve with a craft, he shall on every ember-week pay four pennies, and shall be exempt from the weekly penny, because he be not employed in the Lodge.

r. Item: If a master have a complaint against another master, for having violated the regulations of the craft, or a master against a fellow, or a fellow against another fellow, any master or fellow who is concerned therein shall give notice thereof to the master who presides over the fraternity, and the master who is thereof informed shall hear both parties, and set a day when he will try the cause: and meanwhile, before the fixed or appointed day, no fellow shall avoid the master, nor master drive away the fellow, but render services mutually until the hour when the matter is to be heard and settled. This shall all be done according to the judgement of the craftsmen, which shall be observed accordingly. Moreover, the case shall be tried on the spot where it arose before the nearest master who keeps the Book of Statutes, and in who district it occured.

s. Item: Every Parlirer shall honor his master, be true and faithful to him, according to the rule of Masonry, and obey him with undivided fidelity, as is meet and of ancient usage. So also shall a fellow. And when a traveling fellowcraft desires to travel farther, he shall part from his master and from the Lodge in such wise as to be indebted to no one, and that no man have any grievance against him, as is meet and proper.

t. A travelling fellow, in whatever Lodge he may be employed shall be obedient to his master and to the Parlirer, according to the rule and ancient usage of Masonry, and shall also keep all the regulations and privileges which are of ancient usage in the said Lodge, and shall not revile his master's work, either secretly or openly, in any wise. But if the master infringe upon these regulations, and act contrary to them, then may any one give notice thereof.

u. Every craftsman employing workmen in the Lodge, to whom is confided these statues, and who is duly invested with authority, shall have power and authority in the same over all contentions and matters which pertain to Masonry, to try and punish in his district. All masters, Parlirers, and apprentices, shall obey him.

x. A fellow who has traveled, and is practiced in Masonry, and who is of this fraternity, who wishes to serve a craftsman on a portion of the work, shall not be accepted by that craftsman or master, in any wise for a less term than two years.

y. Item: All masters and fellows who are of this fraternity shall faithfully keep all the points and articles of these regulations, as hereinbefore and hereinafter stands written. But if anyone should perchance violate one of the points, and thereby become punishable, if afterward he be obedient to the regulation, by having compiled with what has been sentenced upon him, he will have done sufficient, and be released from his vow, in regard to the article wherefor he has been punished.

z. The master who has charge of the Book shall, on the oath of the fraternity, have a care that the same be not copied, either by himself or by any other person, or given, or lent, -so that the Book remain intact, according to the resolution of the craftsmen. But if one of the craftsmen, being of this fraternity, have need or cause to know one or two articles, that may any master give him in writing. Every master shall cause these statutes to be read every year to the fellows in the Lodge

Item: If a complaint be made involving a greater punishment as for instance, expulsion from Masonry, the same shall not be tried or judged by one master in his district; but the two nearest masters who are entrusted with the copies of the statutes, and who have authority over the fraternity, shall be summoned by him, so that there may be three. The fellows also who were at work at the place where the grievance arose shall be summoned also, and whatsoever shall be with one accord agreed upon by those three, together with all the fellows, or by a majority thereof in accordance with their oath and best judgement, shall be observed by the whole fraternity of craftsmen.

Item: If two or more masters who are of the fraternity be at variance or discord about matters which do not concern Masonry, they shall not settle these matters anywhere but before Masonry, which shall judge and reconcile them as far as possible, but so that the agreement be made without prejudice to the lords or cities who are concerned in the matter.

1. Now, in order that these regulations of the craft may be kept more honestly, with service to God and other necessary and becoming things, every master who has craftsmen at work in his Lodge, and practises Masonry, and is of this fraternity, and afterward each year four Blapparts; namely, on each ember-week one Blappart or Bohemian to be paid into the box of the fraternity, and each fellow four Blapparts, and so likewise an apprentice who has served his time.

2. All masters and craftsmen who are of this fraternity, who employ workmen in their Lodges, shall each of them have a box, and each fellow shall pay into the box weekly one penny. Every master

shall faithfully treasure up some money and what may be derived from other sources, and shall each year deliver it to the fraternity at the nearest place where a book is kept, in order to provide for God's worship and to supply the necessaries or the fraternity.

3. Every master who has a box, if there be no Book in the same Lodge, shall deliver the money each year to the master who has charge of the Book, and where the Book is there shall also be held divine worship. If a master or fellow dies in a Lodge where no Book is kept, another master or fellow of the said Lodge shall give notice thereof to the master who has a Book; and when he has been informed thereof he shall cause a mass to be said for the repose of the soul of him who has departed, and all the masters and fellows of the Lodge shall assist at the mass and contribute thereto.

4. If a master or fellow be put to any expense or disbursement, for account of the fraternity, and notice be given of how the same occured, to such master or fellow shall be repaid his expenses, be the same small or great, out of the box of the fraternity; if also any one gets into trouble with courts or in other matters, relating to the fraternity, then shall every one, be he master or fellow, afford him aid and relief, as he is bound to do by the oath of the fraternity.

5. If a master or fellow fall sick, or a fellow who is of the fraternity, and has lived uprightly in Masonry, be afflicted with protracted illness and want for food and necessary money, than shall the master who has charge of the box lend him relief and assistance from the box, if he otherwise may, until he recover from his sickness; and he shall afterward vow and promise to restitute the same into the box. But if he should die in such sickness, then so much shall be taken from what he leaves at his death , be it clothing or other articles, as to repay that which has been loaned to him, if so much be there.

These are the Statutes of the Parlires and Fellows

No craftsman or master shall set at work a fellow who commits adultery, or who openly lives in illicit intercourse with women, or who does not yearly make confession, and goes not to the Holy

Communion, according to Christian discipline, nor one who is so foolish as to lose his clothing at play.

Item: if any fellow should wantonly take leave of a Grand Lodge or from another lodge, he should not ask for employment in the said Lodge for a year to come.

Item: If a craftsman or master wishes to discharge a travelling fellow whom he had employed, he shall not do so unless on a Saturday or on a pay evening, so that he may know how to travel on the morrow, unless he be guilty of an offence. The same shall also be done by a fellowcraft.

Item: A travelling fellow shall make application for employment to one but the master of the worker or the Parlirer, neither clandestinely nor openly, without the knowledge and will of the master.

No craftsman or master shall knowingly accept as an apprentice one who is not of lawful birth, and shall earnestly inquire thereof before he accepts him, and shall question such apprentice on his word, whether his father and mother were duly united in lawful wedlock.

Item: No craftsman or master shall promote one of his apprentices as a Parlirer whom he has taken as an apprentice from his rough state, or who is still in his years of apprenticeship.

Neither shall any craftsman or master promote any of his apprentices as a Parlirer whom he has taken from his rough state, notwithstanding he may have served his years of apprenticeship, if he has not travelled for the space of one year.

If any one who has served with a Mason (Murer) comes to a craftsman and wishes to learn of him, the said craftsman shall not accept him as an apprentice unless he serve as such for three years.

No craftsman or master shall take an apprentice from his rough state for a less term than five years.

If, however, it happen that an apprentice should leave his master during the years of his apprenticeship, without sufficient reasons, and does not serve out his time then no master shall employ such apprentice. No fellow shall work with him, nor in any wise keep fellowship with him, until he has served his lawful time with the master whom he left, and has given him entire satisfaction, and brings a certificate from his master aforesaid. No apprentice shall ransom himself from his master unless he intends to marry, with his master's consent, or there be other sufficient reasons which urge him or his master to this measure.

If an apprentice deems that he has not been justly dealt with by his master, in any way they may have agreed upon, then may the apprentice bring him before the craftsmen and masters, who are in that district, so that an explanation and redress may take place as the case may be.

Item: Every master who has a Book in the district of Strasburg, shall pay every year, at Christmas, a half-florin into the box of Strasburg, until the debt is paid which is due to that box.

And every master who has a Book, and whose building is finished, and who has no more work whereon he can employ the fellows, shall send his Book, and the money in his possession, which belongs to the fraternity, to the workmaster at Strasburg.

It was resolved on the day at Regensburg, four weeks after Easter, in the year, counting from God's birth, one thousand four hundred and fifty nine on St. Mark's day, that the workmaster JOST DOTZINGER, of Worms, of the building of our dear Lady's minister, the high chapter of Strasburg, and all of his successors on the same work, should be the supreme judge of our fraternity of Masonry, and the same was also afterward determined on at Spires, at Strasburg, and again at Spires in the year MCCCCLXIV on the 9th day of April.'

Item: Master LORENZ SPENNING, of Vienna, shall also be chief judge at Vienna.

And thus a workmaster or his successors at Strasburg, Vienna, and Cologne these three are the chief judges and leaders of the fraternity; they shall not be removed without just cause, as was determined on, the day at Regensburg, 1459, and at Spires in 1464.

This is the district that belongs to Strasburg; all the country below the Moselle, and Franconia as far as the Thuringian forest, and Babenberg as far as the episcopate at Eichstatten, from Eichstatten to Ulm, from Ulm to Augsburg to the Adelberg and as far as Italy; the countries of Misnia, Thuringia, Saxony, Frankfort, Hesse, and Suabia, these shall be obedient.

Item: To Master LORENZ SPENNING, workmaster of the building of St. Stephen, at Vienna, appertains Lampach, Steiermarch, Hungary, and the Danube downward.

Item: Master STEFFAN HURDER, architect of St. Vincent's at Berne, shall have the district of the Swiss Confederacy.

Item: To Master CONRAD, of Cologen, master of the chapter there, and to all his successors likewise, shall appertain the other districts downward, whatever there be of buildings and Lodges which belong to the fraternity, or may hereafter belong to it.

If any master, Parlirer, fellowcraft, or apprentice acts contrary to any of the hereinbefore or hereinafter written points or articles, and does not keep them collectively or individually, and reliable information be obtained thereof., then he or they shall be summoned before the fraternity, by reason of such violation, and shall be called to account therefor, and shall be obedient, to the correction or penalty which is sentenced upon him, for the sake of the oath and vow which he has pledged unto the fraternity. And if he slights the summons without honest reason, and does not come, he shall yet give what has been sentenced upon him as a penalty for his disobedience, although he be not present. But if he will not do so, he may be brought before ecclesiastical or civil courts at the place where they be held, and may be judged according to what may be right in the matter.

Item: Whoever desires to enter this fraternity, shall promise ever to keep steadfastly all these articles hereinbefore and hereafter written in this Book; except our gracious lord the Emperor, or the King, Princes, Lords, or any other Nobles, by force or right, should be opposed to his belonging to the fraternity; that shall be a sufficient excuse, so that there be no harm therein, but for what he is indebted for to the fraternity, he shall come to an agreement thereon with the craftsman who are in the fraternity.

Although by Christian discipline every Christian is bound to provide for his own salvation, yet it must be duly remembered by the masters and craftsmen whom the Almighty God has graciously endowed with their art and workmanship, to build houses of God and other costly edifices, and honestly to gain their living thereby, that by gratitude their hearts be justly unto true Christian feelings, to promote divine worship, and to merit the salvation of their souls thereby. Therefore to the praise and honour of Almighty God, His worthy Mother Mary, of all her blessed saints, and particularly of the holy four crowned martyrs, and especially for the salvation of the souls of all persons who are of this fraternity, or who may hereafter belong to it, have we the craftsmen of Masonry stipulated and ordained, for us and all our successors, to have a divine service yearly, at the four holy festivals and on the day of the holy four crowned martyrs, at Strasburg, in the minister of the high chapter, in our dear Lady's chapel, with vigils and soul masses, after the manner to be instituted.

It was determined upon the day at Spires, on the ninth day of April, in the year, counting from God's birth, 1464 that the workmaster, JOST DOTZINGER, of Worms, workmaster of the high chapter at Strasburg, shall have an assembly of craftsmen in his district, when three or four masters shall be taken and chosen, to come together on a certain day, as they may agree, and what is there determined on by a majority of those who are so congregated in chapters, and who are then present, and how they may decrease or increase some articles, that shall be kept throughout the whole fraternity.;

The day shall be on St. George's day in the sixty-ninth year.
These are the masters who were present on the day at Spires, on the ninth day of April in the year 1464.

Watson Manuscript
circa 1535

The might of the Father of heaven, with the wisdom of the blessed Son, through the grace of God, and the goodness of the Holy Ghost, that be three persons in one Godhead, be with us at our beginning, and give us grace so to govern us here in this life, that we may come to His blessing, that never shall have ending.

GOOD BRETHREN and Fellows, our purpose is to tell you how and in what manner this worthy science of Masonry was first founded and afterwards how it was maintained and upholden by worthy kings and princes, and many other worshipful men. And also, to them that be here, we will declare the Charges that it belongs to every Free-Mason to keep sure in good faith; and therefore take good heed hereunto, for it is a science that is worthy of being kept, for it is a worthy Craft; and is one of the seven liberal sciences.

The names of the seven liberal sciences are these: The first is "Grammar" that teacheth a man to speak and write truly; the second is "Rhetoric" that teacheth a man to speak well, in subtle terms; the third is "Dialectic," or Logic, that teacheth a man to discern truth from falsehood. The fourth is "Arithmetic," that teacheth a man to reckon and count all kinds of numbers; the fifth is "Geometry" that teacheth a man to mete and measure the earth and all other things, on which science Masonry is grounded. The sixth is "Music" that teacheth the craft of song and voice, of tongue, organ, and harp. The seventh is "Astronomy" that teacheth a man to know the course of the sun, moon, and stars.

THESE be the seven liberal Sciences, the which are all grounded upon one, that is to say Geometry. And this may a man prove that the science of all work is grounded upon Geometry, for it teacheth mete, measure, ponderation, and weight of all manner of things on earth; for there are none that work any science, but he worketh by some measure or weight, and all this is Geometry. Merchants and all

Craftsmen, and others who use the Sciences, and especially the plowmen and tillers of all manner of grains and seeds, planters of vineyards and setters of fruit, none can till without Geometry; for neither in Grammar, Rhetoric, or Astronomy can any man find mete or measure without geometry. Wherefore this science may well be called the most worthy science, for it foundeth all others.

HOW this science was first begun I will now tell you. Before Noah's flood there was a man called Lamech, as it is written in the Bible in the 4th chapter of Genesis. And this Lamech had two wives, the one called Adah by whom he had two sons, one called Jabal and the other Jubal. And his other wife was called Zillah, by whom he had one son Tubal-Cain, and one daughter named Naamah; and these four children founded the beginning of all the sciences in the world. Jabal, the eldest son, found out the science of Geometry; he kept flocks of sheep and lambs in the fields, as it is noted in the chapter aforesaid. His brother Jubal founded the science of Music, in song of tongue, harp, and organ, and trumpet. And the third brother Tubal Cain found the science of smith's craft, in gold, silver, copper, and iron. And their sister Naamah found the craft of weaving. And these persons knowing right well that God would take vengeance for sin, either by fire or water, therefore they writ their several sciences that they had found in ii. pillars of stone, that they might be found after Noah's flood. The one stone was marble that would not burn with fire, and the other called "latres" (latens, laterns, lacerus, &c.) because it would not drown with water. Our intent is now to tell you, how and in what manner these stones were found in which were written these sciences. After the destruction of the world by Noah's flood, as histories affirm, a great clerk called Pythagoras found the one, and Hermes the philosopher (who was Cush's son, who was Shem's son, who was Noah's son) found the other, and was called the Father of wise men. These two found the two pillars in which the sciences were written, and taught them to other men.

AND at the making of the Tower of Babylon masonry was much esteemed. And the king of Babylon that was named Nimrod was a Mason himself, and he loved well Masons and their science, as it is said by Masters of histories. And when the cities of Nineveh, and other cities of eastern Asia, were to be built this Nimrod sent thither three score masons at the request of the King of Nineveh, his cousin, and when he sent them forth he gave them a Charge in this manner. That they should each one be true to the other; that they should love well one another; that they should serve their lord truly for their pay, that the Master may have worship and all that belong to him. And other more Charges he gave them, and this was the first time that a Mason had any Charges of his Craft.

MOREOVER Abraham and Sarah his wife went into Egypt, and there he taught the seven sciences to the Egyptians; and a worthy scholar named Euclid learned right well and was Master of all the vii. sciences; and in his days it befell that the lords and states of the land had so many sons, some by their wives and some by their concubines, for that land is hot and plenteous of generation; and they had not a competent proportion of estates wherewith to maintain their said children, which caused them much care; and the King of that land summoned a great Council to consult how they might provide for their children to live honestly as gentlemen; and they could find no good way. And then they made proclamation throughout all the realm, that if there were any that could inform them therein he should come to them and would be well rewarded for his labours. After this proclamation was made the worthy Clerk Euclid came and said unto the King and the nobles — "If you will accept of me to teach, instruct, and govern your children, I will teach them the vii. liberal sciences whereby they may live honestly as gentlemen. I will do it upon condition that you will grant me and them a commission, that I may have power to rule them, after the manner the science ought to be ruled." The King and all the Council granted him this and sealed the Commission; and then this worthy doctor took to himself these lords' sons and taught them the science of Geometry, and to practise work in stones, of all manner of work that belongeth to building churches, temples, castles, towers, manors, and all other sorts of buildings, and gave them a Charge in this manner: First, that they should be true to the lord that they serve; that they should love well one another; that they should call each other Fellow or Brother, and not servant, knave, or other foul name; that they should truly deserve their pay of their lord, or the master that they served; and that they should ordain the wisest of them to be masters of the work, and neither to chose for love, nor affection, nor greatness, nor richness, to set any in the work that hath not sufficient knowledge or cunning to be master of the work, whereby the Master should be evilly served and they dishonoured; and also that they should call the governor of the work Master, during the time that they work with him, and other more Charges which is too long to tell here. And to all these Charges he made them swear a great Oath, that men used at that time; and he ordained for them reasonable pay that they might live honestly thereby; also that they should assemble themselves together once every year, and consult how they might best work for their lord's profit and their own credit; and correct within themselves him that had trespassed against the science. And thus was the science grounded in Egypt, and that worthy Master Euclid was the first that gave it the name of Geometry the which is now called Masonry.

AND, AFTER that, when the children of Israel were come into the land of Behest which is now called with us the country of Jewry, King David began the temple that is now called Templum Dei, as is called with us the Temple of Jerusalem, and the said King David loved well Masons and cherished them much, and he gave them good wages, and also Charges and manners, as they had learned in Egypt, and other more Charges that you shall hear afterwards. After the decease of King David, Solomon his son finished the said temple that his father had begun, and he sent for Masons out of divers countries and divers lands, and gathered them together so that he had four score thousand workers of stone who were Masons, and he chose out of them three thousand that were ordained to be Masters and governors of the work. And furthermore, there was a king of another region that men called Hiram, and he loved King Solomon well, and he gave him timber for his work. And he had a son named Aman and he was a Master of Geometry, and chief Master of all his gravings, carvings, and all his masons and masonry, as appears in Scripture, in libro primo Regum and chapter 5th. And this Solomon confirmed both the Charges and manners that his father had given to Masons, and thus was the worthy science of Masonry confirmed in the country of Jewry, and city of Jerusalem, and in many other kingdoms.

CURIOUS Craftsmen walked about full wide into other countries, some to learn more craft, and some to teach others that had little skill and cunning. And it befell that there was one curious Mason named Namas Graecas that had been at the building of Solomon's temple and he came into France and there he taught the science of Masonry to men of that land. And there was one of the royal line of France called Charles Martel, and he was a man that loved well such a craft, and he drew to this above said, and learned of him the craft, and took upon him Charges and manners, and afterwards by the providence of God, he was elected King of France, and when he was in his estate he took and helped to make men Masons which before were not; and he gave them both their Charge and manners, and good pay as he had learned of other Masons, and also confirmed a Charter from year to year to hold their Assembly where they would, and cherished them right well, and thus came this famous Craft into France.

ENGLAND in all this time stood void of any Charge of Masonry until St. Alban's time, and in his days the King of England. then a pagan did wall the town (that is now called) St. Albans about. And St. Alban was a worthy Knight and Steward of the King's household, and had the government of the realm, and had also the ordering of the walls of the said town, and he loved and cherished Masons right well, and made their pay right good, for he gave them (3s. a week — 2s. 6d. and 3d. for noon, 3s. 6d. and 3d., etc.), and before that time, throughout all the land, a Mason took but a penny a day, until St. Alban amended it; and he procured them a Charter from the King and his Council, for to hold counsel together, and gave it the name of Assembly, and thereat he was himself, and helped to make men Masons, and gave them a Charge, as ye shall after hear.

BUT it happened soon after the death of St. Alban that there arose great wars in England, which came out of divers nations, so that the goodly rule of Masonry was well nigh destroyed until the days of King Athelstan, who was a worthy King of England, and he brought the land into good rest and peace, and builded many great works, as abbeys, castles, towns, and other buildings, and loved well

Masons; and he had a son named Edwin, that loved Masons, much more than his father, and he was a great practitioner in geometry, and delighted much to talk and commune with Masons and to learn of them skill and cunning, and afterwards for the love he bore to Masons and to their science, he was made a Mason, and he procured for them of the King his father a Charter and Commission to hold every year an Assembly, wheresoever they would within the realm of England, and to correct within themselves all defaults and trespasses that were done within the Craft, and he himself held an Assembly at York, and there he made Masons and gave them the Charges and taught them the manners and commanded that rule to be kept ever after, and also gave them the Charter to keep, and also gave orders that it should be renewed from king to king. And when the Assembly was gathered together he made proclamation, that all Masons who had any writings or understanding of the Charges and manners concerning the said science, that was made before in this land or any other, that they should bring them forth, and when they were viewed and examined, there were found some in French, some in Greek, some in English, and other languages, and the intent and meaning was found all one. And these Charges have been gathered and drawn out of divers antient books and writings, as they were made and confirmed in Egypt by the King and the great Clerk Euclid; and by David and Solomon his son; and in France by Charles Martel who was King of France; and in England by St. Alban; and afterwards by Athelstan and Edward his son, that was king after him.] And he had made a Book thereof, how the Craft was founded, and he himself counselled that it should be read when any Masons should be made, and the Charge given to them. And from that day to this the manners of Masons have been kept and observed in that form, as well as men might observe and govern it.

ADD furthermore at divers Assemblies there hath been added certain Charges more by the best advice of Masters and Fellows. *Tunc unus ex senioribus teneat librum ut ille vel illi potiat vel potiant manus sup librum et tunc precepta deberent Legi.*

EVERY man that is a Mason, take right good heed to these Charges, and if any man find himself guilty of any of them, let him amend himself before God. And in particular, ye that are to be charged, take good heed to keep them right well, for it is perilous and great danger for a man to forswear himself upon "a book" (the Holy Scriptures).

1st — The first Charge is that you be true man to God, and the Holy Church, and that you use neither error nor heresy, according to your own understanding, and to discreet and wise-men's teaching.

2nd — You shall be true liegemen to the King of England without any treason or falsehood, and if you know of any that you amend it privily, if you may, or else warn the King and his Council of it by declaring it to his officers.

3rd — Ye shall be true to one another, that is to say to every Mason of the Craft of Masonry that be allowed Masons, and do unto them as you would they should do unto you.

4th — You shall keep truly all the counsel of Lodge and Chamber, and all other counsel, that ought to be kept by way of Masonry.

5th — Also that you use no thievery, but keep yourselves true.

6th — Also you shall be true to the lord, or Master, that you {556}serve, and truly see that his profit and advantage be promoted and furthered.

7th — And also you shall call Masons your Brethren, or Fellows, and no foul name

8th — And you shall not take in villainy your Fellow's wife, nor desire his daughter, nor servant, nor put him to any discredit.

9th — And also that you pay truly for your meat and drink where you go to table, and that you do not anything whereby the Craft may be scandalised, or receive disgrace.

THESE be the Charges in general that belongeth to every Mason to keep both Masters and Fellows. NOW come I to rehearse certain other Charges singularly, for Masters and Fellows:

1. That no Master take upon him any lord's work, or any other man's work, except he know himself to be of sufficient skill and cunning to perform and finish the same, that so the Craft receive no

slander, but that the lord be well served, and have his work truly done.

2. Also that no Master take any work at unreasonable rates, but so that the lord, or owner, may be truly served with his own goods, and the Master live honestly thereby, and pay his Fellows truly their wages, as the manner is.

3. And also that no Master, nor Fellow, shall supplant another of his work; that is to say, if any Master or Fellow have taken any work to do, and so stands as Master of the said work, you shall not put him out of it, unless he be unable of skill and cunning to perform the same to the end.

4. Also that no Master nor Fellow, take any Apprentice under the term of seven years, and that such apprentice is sufficiently able of body and sound of limbs, also of good birth, free-born, no alien, but descended of a true and honest kindred, and no bondsman.

5. Also that no Mason take any apprentice unless he have sufficient occupation wherein to employ two or three Fellows at the least.

6. Also that no Master or Fellow take any lords' work (in task) that was wont to be journey work.

7. Also that every Master shall give wages to his Fellows according as his work doth deserve, that he be not deceived by false work.

8. Also that none shall slander another behind his back, whereby he may lose his good name, or worldly riches.

9. Also that no Fellow, within the lodge or without it, shall misanswer or reprove another, without cause.

10. Also that every Mason shall reverence his elder brother, and put him to honour.

11. Also that no Mason shall be a common player at cards or dice, or any other unlawful game, or games, whereby the science may be slandered and disgraced.

12. Also that no Fellow at any time go from the Lodge to any town adjoining, except he have a Fellow with him to witness that he was in an honest place, and civil company.

13. Also that every Master and Fellow shall come to the Assembly of Masons, if it he within fifty miles about him, if he have any warning of the same.

14. And if he or they have trespassed or offended against the Craft, all such trespass shall stand there, at the award and arbitration of the Masters and Fellows there (present); they to make them accord if they can, or may, and if they cannot agree then to go to the common law.

15. Also that no Master, nor Fellow, make any mould, rule, or square for any layer, nor set any layer (with) or without to hew any mould stones.

16. And that every Mason shall cherish strange Fellows, when they come out of other countries and set them on work if he can, as the manner is, viz. — if he have no stones, nor moulds, in that place, he shall refresh him with money to supply his necessities until he come to the next Lodge.

17. Also that every Mason shall perform his work truly and not sleightly, for his pay, and serve his lord truly for his wages.

18. Also that every Master shall truly make an end of his work, whether it be by task or journey, viz., by measure or by days, and if he have his pay and all other covenants performed to him by the lord of the work according to the bargain.

19. Also that no Mason shall be a common ribald in lechery to make the Craft slandered.

20. Also that every Mason shall work truly upon the work day, that he may truly deserve his pay, and receive it so he may live honestly on the holiday.

21. And also that you and every Mason shall receive weekly (meekly) and godly (the) pay of your paymaster, and that you shall have due time of labour in the work, and of rest as is ordained by the Master's counsel.

22. And also if any Fellows be at discord you shall truly treat with them to be agreed, shewing favour to neither party, but wisely and truly for both, and that it be in such time that the lord's work be not hindered.

23. And also if you stand Warden, or have any power under the Master whom you serve, you shall be true to him, and a true mediator between the Master and your Fellows, to the uttermost of your power whilst you be in care.

24. Also if you stand Steward either of Lodge, Chambers, or common house, you shall give true accounts to your Fellows, at such time as they have accounts.

25. And also if you have more cunning than your Fellow that stands by you, and see him in danger to spoil his stone, and he asketh counsel of you, you shall inform and teach him honestly, so that the lord's work be not damaged.

THESE Charges that we have now rehearsed to you, and to all others here present, which belongeth to Masons, ye shall well and truly keep to your power. So help you God, and by ye contents of that book. Amen.

The Schaw Statutes
The First Schaw Statute of 1598
Edinburgh, the 28th day of December AD1598.

The Statutes and Ordinances to be observed by all the Master Masons within this realm. Set down by William Schaw, Master of Work to His Majesty and Warden General of the said Craft, with consent of the Masters specified hereafter.

(1) First, they shall observe and keep all the good ordinances established before, concerning the privileges of their craft, by their predecessors of good memory; and especially. They shall be true to one another and live charitably together as becometh sworn brethren and companions of the Craft.

(2) They shall be obedient to their wardens, deacons, and masters in all things concerning their craft.

(3) They shall be honest, faithful, and diligent in their calling, and deal uprightly with their masters, or the employers, on the work which they shall take in hand, whether it be piece-work with meals and pay [task, melt, & fie], or for wages by the week.

(4) None shall undertake any work great or small, which he is not capable to perform adequately, under penalty of forty pounds lawful money or else the fourth part of the worth and value of the work, besides making satisfactory amends to the employers, according as the Warden General may direct or, in the absence of the latter, as may be ordered by the wardens, deacons, and masters of the sheriffdom in which the work is undertaken and carried on.

(5) No master shall take away another master's work after the latter has entered into an agreement with the employer by contract or otherwise, under penalty of forty pounds.

(6) No master shall take over any work at which other masters have been engaged previously, until the latter shall have been paid in full for the work they did, under penalty of forty pounds.

(7) A warden shall be elected annually to have charge of every lodge in the district for which he is chosen by the votes of the masters of the lodges of such district and the consent of the Warden General

if he happens to be present; otherwise the Warden General shall be notified of the election that he may send to the warden-elect necessary directions.

(8) No master shall take more than three 'prentices in his lifetime, without the special consent of all the wardens, deacons, and masters of the sheriffdom in which the to-be-received 'prentice resides.

(9) No master shall take on any 'prentice except by binding him to serve him as such for at least seven years, and it shall not be lawful to make such 'prentice a brother or fellow of the craft until he shall have served other seven years after the completion of his 'prenticeship, without a special license granted by the wardens, deacons, and masters, assembled for that purpose, after sufficient trial shall have been made by them of the worthiness, qualifications and skill of the person desiring to be made a fellowcraft. A fine of forty pounds shall be collected as a pecuniary penalty from the person who is made a fellow of the craft in violation of this order, besides the penalties to be levied against his person by order of the lodge of the place where he resides.

(10) It shall not be lawful for any master to sell his 'prentice to another master, nor to curtail the years of his 'prenticeship by selling these off to the 'prentice himself, under the penalty of forty pounds.

[Item, it sall be no lesum to an maister to sell his prenteiss to ony ether maister not zit to dispense wt the zeiris of his prenteischip be selling yrof to the prenteisses self, ynder th pane of fourtie pounds.]

(11) No master shall take on a 'Prentice without notice to the warden of the lodge where he resides, so that the 'Prentice and the day of his reception may be duly booked.

(12) No 'Prentice shall be entered except according to the aforesaid regulations in order that the day of entry may be duly booked.

(13) No master or fellow of craft shall be received or admitted without there being present six masters and two entered 'prentices, the warden of the lodge being one of the six, when the day of receiving the new fellow of craft or master shall be duly booked and his mark inserted in the same book, with the names of the six admitters and entered 'prentices, as also the names of the intenders [intendaris-instructors] which shall be chosen for every person so

entered in the book of the lodge. Providing always that no man be admitted without an essay and sufficient trial of his skill and worthiness in his vocation and craft.

(14) No master shall engage in any mason work under the charge or command of any other craftsman who has undertaken the doing of any mason work.

(15) No master or fellow of craft shall accept any cowan to work in his society or company, nor send any of his servants to work with cowans, under the penalty of twenty pounds as often as any person offends in this matter.

(16) It shall not be lawful for any entered 'Prentice to undertake any greater task or work for an employer, which amounts to as much as ten pounds, under the penalty just mentioned, to wit twenty pounds, and that task being done he shall not undertake any other work without license of the masters or warden where he dwells.

(17) If any question, strife, or variance shall arise among any of the masters, servants, or entered 'prentices, the parties involved in such questions or debate shall make known the causes of their quarrel to the particular warden and deacon of their lodge, within the space of twenty-four hours, under penalty of ten pounds, to the end that they may be reconciled and agreed and their variances removed by their said warden, deacon, and masters; and if any of the said parties shall remain wilful or obstinate, they shall be deprived f the privilege of their lodge and not permitted to work thereat unto the time that they shall submit themselves to reason according to the view of the said wardens, deacons, and masters.

(18) All masters, undertakers of works, shall be very careful to see that the scaffolds and gangways are set and placed securely in order that by reason of their negligence and sloth no injury or damage [hurt or skaith] may come to any persons employed in the said work, under penalty of their being excluded thereafter from working as masters having charge of any work, and shall ever be subject all the rest of their days to work under or with an other principal master in charge of the work.

(19) No master shall receive or house [resset] a 'Prentice or servant of any other master, who shall have run away from his master's service, nor entertain him in his company after he has received knowledge thereof, under penalty of forty pounds.

(20) All persons of the mason craft shall convene at the time and place lawfully made known to them [being lawchfullie warnit], under penalty of ten pounds.

(21) All the masters who shall happen to be sent to any assembly or meeting, shall be sworn by their great oath that they will neither hide nor conceal any faults or wrongs done to the employers on the work they have in hand, so far as they know, and that under penalty of ten pounds to be collected from the concealers of the said faults.

(22) It is ordained that all the aforesaid penalties shall be lifted and taken up from the offenders and breakers of their ordinances by the wardens, deacons, and masters of the lodges where the offenders dwell, the moneys to be expended ad pios usus (for charitable purposes) according to good conscience and by the advice of such wardens, deacons, and masters.

For the fulfilling and observing of these ordinances, as set down above, the master convened on the aforesaid day bind and obligate themselves faithfully. Therefore they have requested their said Warden General to sign these ordinances by his own hand in order that an authentic copy hereof may be sent to every particular lodge within this realm.

(Signed) WILLIAM SCHAW,
Master of the Work

The Schaw Statutes
The Second Schaw Statute of 1599

As the document is rather long, the several items have been somewhat condensed and placed in an ordered sequence. The numbering of the paragraphs is done for purposes of convenient reference:

(1) Edinburgh shall be, in the future as in the past, the first and principal lodge in Scotland; Kilwinning, the second "as is established in our ancient writings;" and Stirling shall be the third lodge, "conformably to the old privileges thereof."

(2) The warden within the bounds of Kilwinning and other places subject to their lodge, shall be elected annually by a majority [be monyest] of the masters of the lodge, on the twentieth day of December, in the Kirk of Kilwinning. Immediately after election, the Warden General must be notified who was chosen warden.

(3) Agreeably to "former ancient liberties," the warden of Kilwinning shall be present at the election of wardens within the limits of the lower ward of Cliddisdale, Glasgow, Ayr, and the district of Carrik. Furthermore, the warden and deacon of Kilwinning shall have authority to convene the wardens within the indicated jurisdiction, when anything of importance is to be done, such meetings to be held at Kilwinning or any other place in the western part of Scotland included in the described bounds, as the warden and deacon of Kilwinning may appoint.

(4) The warden of each and every lodge shall he answerable to the presbyters of the sheriffdom for all offences committed by masons subject to these lodges. One third of all fines imposed for offences shall be applied to charitable [godlie] uses.

(5) The wardens together with the oldest masters, up to the number of six, of every lodge shall hold an annual investigation of offences committed and try all offenders to the end that proper punishment may be meted out conformably to equity and justice and good conscience, according to traditional procedure.

(6) The warden of Kilwinning shall appoint six worthy and perfect masons, well known to the craft as such, to inquire into the qualifications of all the masons within the district, as regards their skill and knowledge of the trade and their familiarity with the old traditions, to the end that the warden [and] deacon may be answerable thereafter for all such persons within his district and jurisdiction.

(7) Authority is given to the warden [and] deacon of Kilwinning to exclude from the lodges of the district all persons who wilfully fail to live up to "all the acts and ancient statutes set down from time immemorial," also all who are ."disobedient to their church, craft, council and other statutes and acts to be promulgated hereafter for good order."

(8) The warden and deacon, together with the masters of the district [quarter maisteries] shall elect a well known notary [constitut ane famous notar] as clerk and secretary [scryb] who shall make out and sign all indentures, discharges, and other writings whatsoever, pertaining to the craft, and no writ, title or other evidence shall be admitted by the warden and deacon, except it shall have been executed by this clerk and signed by him.

(9) All the acts and statutes made by the predecessors of the masons of Kilwinning shall be observed faithfully and kept by the craft in all time coming; 'prentices and craftsmen shall be admitted and entered hereafter only in the Kirk of Kilwinning, as their parish and second lodge, and all entry-banquets of 'prentices and fellows of craft shall be held in the lodge of Kilwinning.

(10) Every fellow of craft, at his entry, shall pay to his lodge ten pounds to go for the banquet, and ten shillings for gloves; before admission he shall be examined by the warden [and] deacon and the district masters in the lodge as to his knowledge [memorie] and skill, and he also shall perform an assigned task to demonstrate his mastery of the art.

(11) Every 'prentice, before he is admitted, shall pay six pounds to be applied to the common banquet.

(12) The warden and deacon of the second lodge of Scotland, to wit Kilwinning, shall obligate by oath all masters and fellows of craft within the district not to associate with cowans nor work with them, neither to permit this to be done by their servants or 'prentices.

The Schaw Statutes (Second)

(13) The warden of the lodge of Kilwinning, being the second lodge of Scotland, once in each year, shall examine every fellow craft and 'prentice, according to the vocation of each, as to his skill and knowledge; those who have forgotten any points they have been taught shall pay fines.

St. Clair Charters
First Charter 1601
Second Charter 1628

Charter Granted by the Masons of SCOTLAND to WILLIAM ST CLAIR of ROSLIN in 1601

Be it kend till all men be thir present letters ws Deacons Maistres and freemen of the Masons within the realme of Scotland with express consent and assent of Wm Schaw Maister of Wark to our Souane Lord ffor sa meikle as from aige to aige it has been observit amangis that the Lairds of Rosling has ever been Patrons and Protectors of us and our priviledges likeas our predecessors has obey'd and acknowledged them as Patrones and tectoris while that within thir few years throwch negligence and sleuthfulness the samyn has past furth of vse whereby not only has the Laird of Rosling lyne out of his just rycht but also our hail craft has been destitute of ane patron and protector and overseer qlk has genderit manyfauld corruptions and imperfections, baith amangis ourselves and in our craft and has given occasion to mony persones to conseve evill opinioun of ws and our craft and to leive off great enterprises of policie be reason of our great misbehaviour wtout correction whereby not only the committers of the faults but also the honest men are disapoyntit of their craft and ffeit. As lyikwayes when divers and sundrie contraversies falls out amangis ourselfs thair follows great and manyfald inconvenientis through want of ane (Patron and Protector) we not being able to await upon the ordinar judges and judgement of this realme through the occasioun of our powertie and langsumness of process for remeid qrof and for keeping of guid ordour amangis us in all tymes cumyng, and for advancement of our craft and vocatioun within this realme and furthering ofpolicie within the samyn We for ourselves and in name of our haill bretherene and craftismen with consent foresaid agrees and consents that Wm Sinclar now of Rosling for himself & his airis purchase and obtene at ye hands of our Souane Lord libertie fredome and jurisdictioun vpone us and our successors in all tymes cummyng as patrons and judges to us and the haill fessoris of our craft wtin this realme quhom off we have power and commission sua that hereafter we may acknawlege him and his airis as our patrone and judge under our Souerane Lord without ony kind of appellation or declynyng from his judgement with power to the said Williame and his airis to depute judges ane or mae under him and to use sick ampill and large jurisdictione upon us and our successors als weill as burghe as land as it shall pleise our Souerane Lord to grant to him & his airis.

William Schaw, Maistir of Wark.
Edinburgh - Andro Symsone Jhone Robesoune
St Androse - *******

Hadingtoun - P. Capbell takand ye burdyng for Jon. Saw, J. Vallance William Aittoun Achiesone Heavin - Georg Aittoun Jo. Fwsetter Thomas Petticrif Dunfermling – Robert Pest Thomas Weir mason in Edr. Thomas Robertsoun wardane of the Ludge of Dunfermling and Sanct Androis and takand the burding upon him for the brethren of the Mason Craft within they Lwdges and for the Commissioners efter mentionat viz. David Skowgall Alexander Gilbert and David Spens for the Lwdge of Sanct Androis Andrew Alisone and Archibald Angous Commissionaris for the Lwdge of Dwmfermling and Robert Baize of Haddington with our handis led on the pen be the notaris underwritten at our commandis because we can nocht write. Ita est Laurentius Robertsoun notarius publicus ad praemissa requisitus de specialibus mandatis dict. personarum scribere nescien. ut aseruerunt testan. manu mea propria. (Ita est) Henricus Banna(Tyne) connotarius ad premissa (de mandatis) antedictarum personarum (scribere nescientium ut aseruerunt teste) manu mea propria.

Charter Granted by the Masons of Scotland to Sir WILLIAM ST CLAIR in 1628

Beit kend till all men be thir present letters ws the Deacones Masteris friemen of the Maissones and Hammermen within the kingdome of Scotland That forsameikill as from aidge to aidge it has been observet amangis us and our predecessors that the Lairdis of Rosling has ever been patrons and protectors of us and our priviledgis Likeas our predecessors has obeyit reverencet and acknowledget them as patrons and protectors qrof they had letters of protection and vtheris richtis grantit be his Maties most noble progenitors of worthy memorie qlkis with sindrie vtheris of the Lairdis of Rosling his writtis being consumet and brunt in ane flame of fire within the Castle of Rosling in an ..... The consumation and burning qrof being clearly knawin to us and our predecessors deacons maisteris and freemen of the saidis vocations, and our protection of the samyn and priviledgis thereof (be negligence) and slouthfulness being likely to pass furth of us where throw not only wald the Lairdis of Rosling lyne out of their just richt but also our hail craftis wald haifbene destitute of ane patrone protector and oversear quhilk wald engenner monyfald imperfectionis and corruptionis baith amangis ourselves and in our craft and give occasione to mony persones to conceive evill opinioun of us and our craft and to leave af many and grit enterpryces ofpolicie whilk wald be vndertaken if our grit misbehaviour were suffered to goe on without correctioun For remeid qrof and for keeping of good ordour amangis us in all time coming and for advancement of our craft and vocation within his Hienes kingdom of Scotland and furdering of policie yaireintill the maist pairt of our predecessors for themselves and in name and behalfe of our bretherene and craftsmen with express advice and consent of William Schaw Maister of Wark to Hienes umqle darrest father of worthy memorie all in ane voce agreit consentit and subseryvet that William Sinclar of Rosling father to Sir William Sinclar now of Rosling for himself and his airis should purches and obtain at the hands of his Majestie libertie freedome and jurisdictioun upon us and our predecessors deacons maisteris and freemen of the saidis vocation, as patrones and judges to us and the haill professors thereof within the said kingdom qrof they had power and commission sua that they and we micht yairafter acknowledge him and his airis as patrone and judge under our Soverane Lord without any kind of appellation or declinatour from thair judgement forever, as the said agreement subscryvet be the said Mr of Wark and our predecessors at mare length proportis In the whilk office priviledge and jurisdictioun over us and our said (voca)tioun the said William Sinclar of Rosling ever continuit to his going to Ireland qr he presently reamanes sen the quhilk (time) of his departure furth ofthis realme there are very many corruptiounes and imperfectiounes risen and ingennerit baith amangis ourselfis and in our saidis vocatiounes in defect of ane patrone and oversear over us and the samyn Sua that our saidis vocatiounes are altogether likely to decay And now for safety thereof we having full experience of the efauld good skill and judgement whilk the said Sr William Sinclar now of Rosling has in our said craft and vocatioun and for reparation of the ruines and manifold corruptiounes and enormities done be unskilfull persones thereintill WE all in ane voce have ratified and approven and be thir presentis ratifies and approves the foresaid former letter ofjurisdictioun and libertie made and subr be our brethrene and his Hienes umqle Mr of Wark for the time to the said Williame Sinclar of Rosling father to the said Sr William whereby he and his airis are acknowledget as our patrone and judge under our Soverane Lord over us and the haill professors of our said vocatioun within this his Hienes kingdom of Scotlande without any appelation or declinator from their judgements in ony (time hereafter) forever And further we all in ane voce as said is of new have made constitute and ordainit and be thir presentis makis constitutes and ordanes the said Sir William Sinclar now of Rosling and his airis maill our only patrones protectors and overseers under our Soverane Lord to us and our successors deacons maisteris and freemen of our saidis vocatiounes of Masons hammermen within the haile kingdome of Scotland and of our haille priviledges and jurisdictiounes belonging thereto wherein he his father and their predecessors Lairdis of Rosling have been in use of possessioun thir many aidges bygain with full power to him and them be themselves thair wardens and deputis to be constitute be them to affix and appoint places of meeting for keeping of good ordour in the said craft als oft and sua oft as need shall require all and sundry persones that may be knawin to be subject to the said vocatioun to be called absentis to amerciat transgressuris to punish unlawes casualities and vtheris duties whatsomever pertaining and belonging or that may fall to be pait be whatsomever persone or persones subject to the said craft to aske crave receive intromet with and uplift and the samyn to their own proper use to apply deputtis under them in the said office with clerkis seruandis assisteris and all other officers and memberis of court needfull to make create substitute and ordain for whom they shall be holden to answer all and sundry plentis actions and causes pertaining to the said craft and vocation and against whatsomever person or persones professors thereof to hear discuss decerne and decyde acts duties and sentences thereupon to pronunce And the samyn to due execution to cause be put and generallie all and sundrie other priviledges liberties and immunities whatsomever concerning the said craft to doe use and exerce and cause to be done and exercet and keipit siklyke and als freely in all respects as any vyeris thair predecessors has done or might have done themselves in anytime bygane freely quietly well and in peace but any revocatioun obstacle impediment or again calling quhtsomevir.

In witness of the qlke thing to thir presenttis wtin be Alexander Aikinheid servitor to Andrew Hay wrytter we have subt thir nts with our handis at . . The Ludge of Edinburgh. - William Wallace decon John Watt Thomas Patersone The Ludge of Glasgow. - John Boyd deakin. Robert Boyd ane of the mestres. Hew Douok deikon of the Measounes and Vrichtis off Ayre and George Lid(ell) deacan of quarimen and nov quartermaster.

The Ludge of Stirlinge. - John Thompsone James Rind The Ludge of Dunfermlinge. - (Robert Alisone one of the masters of Dunfermling) The Ludge of Dundee. - Robert Strachoune master Robert Johnstone Mr of (-) David Mesone Mr of (-) Thomas Fleming wardane in Edinburgh and Hugh Forrest with our hands att the pen led be the notar under subd for us at our command because we cannot wryt. A. Hay notarius asseruit. Robert Caldwell in Glasgow with my hand at the pen led be the notar under subscrywand for me because I cannot writt myself. J. Henrysone notarius asseruit. I John Serveite Mr of ye Craftis in Stirling with my hand att ye pen led be the notar under subscryvand for me because I cannot writt J. Henrysone notarius asseruit. I John Burne ane of the mris. of Dumfermling with my hand att the pen led be the notar under subscrywand for me at my command because I cannot writ myself. J. Henrysone notarius asseruit. David Robertson ane of ye mesteris Andrew Welsone master and Thomas (W)elsone varden of the sed Ludg of Sant Androis Andrew Wast and David Quhyit maisteris in Dundee with our hands att the pen led be the notar under subscryvand att our commands because we cannot writt. Thomas Robertson notarius asseruit.

Harleian Manuscript
The New Articles and Apprentice Charge
circa early 17th Century

The New Articles

(1) 26. No person (of what degree soever) bee accepted a Free-Mason unless he shall have a lodge of five Free Masons; at least where of one to be a Master or Warden, of that limitt or devision, wherein such lodge shall be kept, and another of the trade of Free Masonry.

(2) 27. That noe p'son shall be accepted a Free Mason but such as are of able body, honest parentage, good reputation, and observers of the laws of the land.

(3) 28. That noe p'son hereafter be accepted a Free Mason, nor shall be admitted into any Lodge or Assembly until hee hath brought a certificate of the time of accep'con from the Lodge yt accepted him, unto the master of that limitt and devision where such Lodge was kept which say'd Master shall enrole the same in parchment in a role to he kept for that purpose, to give an account of all such Accep'cions at every general Assembly. "See the acct. of such Roll at York, Ch. X."

(4) 29. That every person whoe now is Free Mason shall bring to the Master a note of the time of his accep'tion, to the end the same may be enrolled in such priority of place of the p'son shall deserve and to ye end the whole Company and Fellows may the better know each other.

(5) 30. That for the future the say'd Society, Company, and Fraternity, of Free Masons shall be regulated and govern'd by one Master, and Assembly, and Wardens, as ye said Company shall think fitt to chose at every yearly general Assembly.

(6) 31. That no p'son shall be accepted a Free Mason, or know the secrets of the said Society, until he hath first taken the Oath of secrecy hereafter following: — I, A.B., doe in the presence of Almighty God and my Fellows and Brethren here present, promise and declare that I will not at any time hereafter, by any act or circumstance whatsoever, directly or indirectly, publish, discover, reveale, or make knowne, any of the secrets, priviledges, or counsells, of the Fraternity or Fellowship of Free Masons, which at this time, or

at any time hereafter, shall be made knowne unto mee. So helpe mee God, and the holy contents of this booke.

The Charge Belonging to an Apprentice

1. You shall truly honour God and his Holy Church, the King, your Master, and Dame, you shall not absent yourself but with the license of both, or one of them, from their service by day or night.

2. You shall not purloin or steal, or be privy, or accessory to the purloining or stealing, to the value of sixpence, from them, or any of them.

3. You shall not commit adultery, or fornication, in the house of your Master, with his wife, daughter, or maid.

4. You shall not disclose your Master's or Dame's counsels, or secrets, which they have imparted to you, nor what is to be concealed, spoken, or done within the precincts of their house, by them or either of them, or by Free Masons.

5. You shall reverently behave yourself to all Free Masons, not using cards, or dice, or any other unlawful games, Christmas excepted.

6. You shall not haunt, or frequent any taverns, alehouses, or such as go into any of them, except when your Master's business, or Dame's, their, or any of their affairs, or without their or any of their consent.

7. You shall not commit adultery or fornication in any man's house, where you shall be at table or at work.

8. You shall not marry or contract yourself to any woman during your Apprenticeship.

9. You shall not steal any man's goods, but especially your said Master's, or any of his Fellow Masons', or suffer any one to steal their goods, but shall hinder it if you can, and if you cannot, then you shall acquaint your said Master, and his Fellows presently.

Sloane Ms. No. 3848
(A.D. 1646.)
A transcript from the Original in the British Museum

THE might of ye Father of Heaven, wth ye wisdome of ye glorious sonne; through ye goodness of ye holy gost; yt bee three psons in one god, &c. bee wth us at or begininge; and give us grace soe to govefne us in our liveinge; yt wee may come to his blisse yt never shall have endinge.

Good Brethren & Fellowes our purpose is to tell you, how & in what manner this Craft of Masonrie was begun, and afterwards founded by worthy Kings and Princes & many other wortt men; and also to ym that be heare; wee will declare to ym the charge yt doth belonge to every true Mason to keepe: For good sooth if you take heede therunto it is well Worthie to bee well kept, for a worthie Craft and curious science. For there bee seaven liberall sciences, of ye wch it is one. The first is Grammer; yt teacheth a man to speake truth and write truly; The second is Rethoricke yt teacheth a man to speak faire & in subtill tearmes. The third Loggick, yt teacheth to disearne truth from falcehood. The fourth is Arithmeticke; yt teacheth to account & recount all manner of numbers; The fift is called Geomeetree; and it teacheth ye meate & measure of ye earthe; and other things, which science is Masonrie ; The sixt is Musicke; wch teacheth songe &; voyce of tongue; of organs & harpe; The seaventh is called Astronomie; that teacheth to know ye course of sonne & moone; and othet Ornaments of ye heavens; These 7 liberall Sciences, ye which seaven bee all one Science ; That is to say Geometry, Thus may a man proue, yt all Science in ye world bee found by Geometry; for it teacheth meate and measure ponderation & waight of all manner of kind earth; And there is noe man yt worketh by any Craft but hee worketh by some measure ; and noe man yt byes and sells, but by measure & weight, and all Geometriarians & Crafttsmen and Merchants find noe other of ye Seaven Sciences; and especially Plowmen and tillars of all manner of graine; both of cornes seeds vines plaints; sellers of all other fruites; For Gramer neither Astronomie; nor any of all these can finde a man one measure or meate; wthout Geometry wherefore I thinke that science most worthy that findeth all others; How this worthy science was first begun I shall tell you; before Noes flood was a man called Lameth as it is written in ye 4 Chaptr of Gene, and this Lameth had two wives, ye one was called Adar, ye other Sella; and by the first wife Adar hee begott 2 sonnes. The one was called Jabell ye other Juball; And by ye other wife hee had a sonne & a daughter; and these foure children found ye beginninge of all Craft in ye world; This Jabell was ye elder soone; and hee found ye Craft of Geometry; and he depted flockes of Sheep & lambes in ye field, And hee first wrought house of stone & tree, and it is notes in ye Chapt aforesaide yt his brother Juball found musicke of Songe harpe & Orgaines; The 3 Brother Tuball found out Smiths Crafts of Iron & steele; and there sister found weavinge ; and these children did knowe that god would take vengencc for sinne eather by fire or water; wherefore they writ ye Sciences wch weare found in 2 pillers of stone ; yt ye might bee found after ye flood; The one stone was called marble that cannot burne wth fire; The other was called Letera that cannot drowne wth water; Our intent is to tell you truly how & in what manner these stones weare found; where these Crafts weare written in Greeke; Hermines that was sonne to Cus; & Cus was sonne to Shem, wch was ye sonne of Naoth; The same Hermenes was afterwards Hermes; the Father of wise men and hee found out ye 2 pillers of stone where ye Sciences weare written & taught ym forth; And at ye makeinge of ye Towre of Babilon there Was the craft of Masonrie first found & made much of, yo Kinge of Babilon wch was called Hembroth or Membroth hee was a mason and loued well ye craft; as it is saide with ye maistr of ye Stories; And when ye Citie of Ninivie & other cities of East Azia should bee made. The Kinge of Babilon sent thither sixe at ye desire of the King of Ninive his cozen; and they went forth, and hee gaue hm a Charge on this maner, That ye should bee true & line truly together; and that ye should serue there lord truly for their payment; for that he might have worpp for sendinge ym & other Charges hee gaue them; and this was ye first time yt any Mason had any Charge of his Craft; Moreovr when Abraham & Sara his wife went into Egypt there weare taught the seaven sciences unto Egyptians; And hee had a worthy Scholler called Euchild and hee Learned right well and was Maistr of all the 7 Sciences; And it befell in his daies that ye Lords and States of ye Realme; had soe many soones yt ye had begotten; some by there wives; & some by Ladies of the Realme; For y' Land is a holy Land and plenished generacon; And ye had noe competent Liveige for there children; wherefore ye made much sorrowe: And ye King of ye Land made greate counsell, & a pliaint to knowe how ye might finde there Children meanes, & they could finde noe good wages; And caused a cry to bee made throughout ye Realme; yt if there weare any man that could informe him; yt hee should come to him and bee well rewarded; and hold himselfe well apaide; and after this cry was made came this worthy Clarke Euchild and said to ye Kinge and all his great Lords if you will have yor children govrned and taught honestly as gentlemen should bee; under condicon that you will grant ym and mee a commission; yt I may haue power to rule them honestly as theise Sciences ought to be ruled; and ye Kinge wth his councell granted them; & sealed yt commission; And then yt worthy Docter tooke the Lordes sonnes and taught ym this Science of Geometry in practice to worke masonrie all manner of worthy workes; yt belongeth to buildinge of castles all manner corts temples and churches; wth all other buildings; and hee gaue ym charge in this manner; First that ye should bee true to ye Kinge and to yo Lords ye served; & that they should love well together; and be true one to another; & that they should call one another fellowes; and not servants no knave nor other foul names; and that ye should truly serue there paymt to ye lord that others serve; and that ye should ordaine ye wisest of them to bee made Mr. of ye Lords worke; and neither for love great lineinge nor riches; to sett another that hath little cunninge to bee Mr. of ye lords worke wherebye hee should bee evilly served or they ashamed; and that ye should call the govrnor of ye worke Mr. of ye worke whilst ye worke wth him; & many other charges which weare too long to tell; and to all these charges hee made ym sweare the great oath men used in yt time; and ordained for them reasonable payment; yt ye might live by it honestly: & alsoe that ye should come & assemble wth others that ye might have councell in these crafts; yea might worke best to serve there lord; for his pfitt and worspp and to correcte themselves if ye had trespased; and thus ye craft of Geometree was gourned there; and yt worthy Mr. gave it ye name of Geometry and it is called masonrie in this Land long after the Children of Israeli were come into the land of .... It is now amongst us in ye countryof Jerasalem Kinge David begaun the temple of Jerusalem that is wth them templum Dei; And ye said King David loved masons well; and cherished them; and gave ym good payment. And hee gave ym charges that ye shall heare afterwards; and after ye decease of King David; Solomon yt was sonne to King David pformed out ye Temple his Father had begun: and hee sent afterwards masons of divers Lands; and gathered ym together; soe yt hee had fourscore thousand workers of stone; and they weare named masons; and he had 3 thousand of them; wt which weare ordained Mrs. — and Gov'nors of yt worke, and there was a King of another Region yt men called Hyram and he loved well Kinge Solomon; and gave him timber for his worke; and hee had a son that was named Aynon & hee was Mr. of Geometry; and he was chiefe Mr. of all his masons ; and Mr. of all his graued workes; and of all other masons that belongeth to ye Temple; & this witnesseth the Bible in libro 2. *Solo,* capite 5. And this Sonne Solomon confermed both charges & manners; yt his father had given to masons; and thus was ye worthy craft of masons confermed in ye country of Jerusalem; and in many other Kingdomes Glorious Craftsmen walkeing abroade into divers Countres; some because of learning more craft; and other some to teach there craft; and so it befell that a curious workman; who was named Nimus Greacus & had beene at ye makeinge of Solomons Temple; and came into France; and there taught ye craft of masonrie; to ye men of France that was named Charles Martill; hee loved well this craft and drew to him this Ninias Greacus; and learned of him ye craft; and tooke upon him ye charges and mannrs. and afterwardes by ye grace of god hee was elected Kinge of France; and when hee was in his Estate hee tooke many masons; and made masons there yt weare none; and sett ym in worke and gave ym both charges and mannrs & good payment; wch he had learned of other masons ; and conferred ym a charter from yeare to yeare to hold there assembly, and thus came ye craft into France; all this while England was voyde, both of any charge or masonrie; vntill ye time of St. Albons; and in his time ye King of England that was a Pagan; and hee walled ye Towne wot is now called St. Albons; and soe in Albon's time a worthie Knight; and chiefe Stewarde to ye King and had gou'mt of ye Realme; and alsoe of makinge ye Towne Walles; and hee loved masons well; & cherished them; & made there paymt right good standinge wages, as ye Realme did require. For he gave ym every weeke iijs. vjd. to there double wages; before yt time through all ye Land a masoun tooke but id. a day, and next to yt time yt St. Albons mended it; hee gott ym a charter from ye King and his councell; and gave ym charges as you shall heare hereafter. After ye decease of St. Albons there came greivous wars into England; through nations ; soe yt ye good rule of masonrie was destroyed; untill ye time of King Athelstone; yt was a worthy King in England and hee brought ye Land into good rest & peace againe; and hee builded many great workes & Castles and Abbies; and many other Buildings ; and hee loued masons very well; & hee had a Sonne yt was named Ladrian; and hee loued masons much more then his Father. For hee was full of practice in Geometry; wherefore hee drew himselfe to commune wth masons; and to Learne of ym ye craft; and afterwards for ye Love hee had to masons; and to ye craft yt hee was made mason himselfe.

And hee gott of his Father ye King a Charter, and a commission to hold every year an Assembly where they would wthin ye Realme; and to correcte wtt ym selves statutes and trespasses; if it weare done wthin ye crafte; and hee held himself assembly at York and there hee made Masons, and gave ym Charges and taught them the mannrs of Masons; and Commanded that rule to bee holden evr after: And to them took ye charter & Commission to keepe; and ordained yt it should be ruled from King to King : when this assembly was gathered together; hee caused a cry to be made; yt all Masons both yong & old yt had any writinge or understandinge of ye charges that weare made before in this land, or in any other Land; yt ye should shew ym forth and there was some in French, some in Greeke, & some in English; and some in other Languages; and ye intent thereof was found; & thereof hee commanded a booke to be made how ye crafte was first found & made, & commanded that yt should bee read and told when any Masons should bee made; and to give him his charge; and from that time untill his time Masonrie untill this day hath beene kept in yt forme & ordr as well as men might gourne ye same; and urthermore at dyurs assembles hath beene put to and aded certaine Charges; more by ye best advices; of Mastrs and Fellowes.
Heare followeth the worthie and godly oath of Masons. Every man that is a Masonn take Heede right well; to this charge; if you fmde

yorselfe guilty of any of these; yt you amend you; againe especially you yt are to bee charged take good heed that you may keepe this charge; for it is a great perrill for a man to forseweare himselfe on a book.

1. The first charge is that you shall bee true man to god ; and ye holy Church; and that you vse noe heresie nor errour by yor vnderstandinge or by teaching of a discreet man.

2. Alsoe you shall be true Leighman to the King wttout treason or falshood, and that you shall knowe noe treason, but that you amend it if you may ; or else warne the King or ye Counsell thereof.

3. Alsoe you shall bee true one to another that is to say to every Mr & fellowe of ye trust of Masonrie ; yt bee Masons allowed; & that you doe to them as you would ye should doe to you.

4. Alsoe that no Mason bee thiefe in companie soe far forth as you shall knowe.

5. Alsoe every Mason shall keepe true Counsell of Lodge and Chamber; and all other Counsell that ought to bee kept by ye way of Masonrie.

6. Alsoe that you shall bee true vnto ye Lorde & Mr that you serue; and truly to see for his pfitt & advantage.

7. Alsoe yt you doe noe vilanie in that house whereby the Craft shall bee slandered.

These bee Charges in generall wch every Mason should hould both Maistrs and fellowes.

Nowe I will rehearse other Charges in singular for Mrs and fellowes.

1. First that noe Maister shall take upon him any Lords worke or other worke, but that hee knowe himselfe able & cunninge to pforme the

same, soe yt the Craft haue noe disworpp but that ye Lord may bee serued & that truly.

2. Alsoe that noe Maister take any worke but he take it reasonable, soe yt ye Lord may bee truly serued wtli his owne good; & ye Mr to liue honestly; and to pay his fellowes truly there pay as the manner of ye Craft doth require.

3. Alsoe that noe Maister nor fellowe shall supplant others of there worke; (that is to say) if ye haue taken a worke, or stand Mr of a Lords worke you shall not put him out of it; if hee bee able of Cunning to pforme ye same.

4. Alsoe that noe Mr nor fellowe take any apprentize ; to bee alowed his apprentize; but for seaven yeares; and yt ye apprentize bee alsoe of his birth and limbs as hee ought to bee.

5- Alsoe that noe Mr nor fellowe take alowance te bee made Mason wthout ye asent of his fellowes yt at the least five or sixe ; and that hee that shall bee made Mason; to bee able our all syers; (yt is to say) that hee be free borne, and of good Kinred and noe bondman; and yt hee haue his right Limes as a man ought to haue.

6. Alsoe That noe Mr put a Lordsman to taske yt is vsed to goe to Joyrney.

7. Also every Mason shall giue noe pay to his fellowes but as hee shall diserne; soe that hee bee not deceived by falce workemen.

8. Also That noe fellowe slander other falsly behifid his backe ; to make him loose his good name or worldy goods.

9. Alsoe yt noe fellowe wthin the Lodge or wthout answer another vngodlily wthout reasonable cause.

10. Also ev'ry Mason shall pferr his elder and put him to worshipp.

11. Also that noe Mason shall play at Hazards or any other unlawful game; whereby they may bee slandered.

12. Alsoe that noe Mason shall bee a common Rybold in lecherie; to make ye Craft slandered; and that noe fellowe goe into ye Towne where is a Lodge of fellowes; wtliout a fellowe wth him; that may beare him witnes; that hee was in honest Companie:

13. Alsoe yt every Mr and fellowe come to ye assembly if it bee wthin fiftie myles; about him; if hee have any warninge; and to stand at ye reward of Mrs and fellowes.

14. Alsoe that eu'rye Maister and fellowe if he have trespassed, shall stand at ye reward of Mrs & fellowes to make them acord if ye may, (but if ye may not to goe to ye Common Lawe.

15. Alsoe That noe Mason make moulds square or rule to any rough Lyers.

16. Alsoe That noe Mason sett noe layes wthin a Lodge or wthout to have mould stone wth noe mould of his owne workinge.

17. Alsoe when ye come our ye country to sett them on worke as ye manner is (yt is to say) if they have mould stones in place ; he shall sett him a fortnight in worke ; & giue him his hire ; and if there bee noe stones for him ; Then refresh him wth some money ; to bring him to ye next Lodge.

18. Alsoe you shall & evruye Mason shall serue truly ye workes; and truly make an end of yor workes, bee it taske or Joyrney ; if you may haue yor pay as you ought to haue ; These Charges that we have rehearsed & all other yt belongeth to Masonrie you shall keepe ; to ye vttermost of yor knowledge ; Soe helpe you god & by the Contents of this booke.

Finis p me Eduardu Sankey
decimo sexto die Octobris Anno Domini 1646.

Inigo Jones Manuscript
circa 1655

THE MIGHT of the FATHER of HEAVEN, and the Wisdom of the Glorious SON, through the Grace and Goodness of the HOLY GHOST, three Persons and One GOD; Be with us and Give us Grace so to Govern us here in our living, that we may come to his Bliss that never shall have Ending. AMEN.

GOOD BRETHREN and FELLOWS, Our Purpose is to tell you how and in what manner this Worthy Craft of MASONRY, was begun; And afterward, how it was kept and Encouraged by Worthy KINGS and Princes, and by many other Worthy Men. AND ALSO to those that be here; We will Charge by the Charges that belongeth to Every FREEMASON to keep; FOR in good Faith, If they take Good heed to it, its worth to be well kept FOR MASONRY is a Worthy Craft, and a curious SCIENCE, and One of the LIBERAL sciences.

THE Names of the Seven liberal sciences are these:

I GRAMMAR, and that teacheth a Man to Speak and write truly.
II RHETORICK and that teacheth a Man to Speak fair, and in soft terms.
III LOGICK, and that teacheth a Man to discern truth from falsehood. IV ARITHMETICK, which teacheth a Man to Reckon, and Count all manner of Numbers.
V GEOMETRY, and that teacheth a Man the Mete and Measure of the Earth, and of all other things; which SCIENCE is Called MASONRY.
VI MUSICK, which Gives a Man Skill of Singing, teaching him the ART of Composition; & playing upon Diverse Instruments, as the ORGAN and HARP methodically.
VII ASTRONOMY, which teacheth a Man to know the Course of Sun, Moon and Starrs.

NOTE I pray you, that these Seven are contain'd under Geometry, for it teacheth Mett and Measure, Ponderation and

Weight, for Every thing in and upon the whole Earth for you to know; That every Crafts man, works by Measure. He buys or sells, is by weight or Measure. Husbandmen, Navigators, Planters and all of them use GEOMETRY for neither GRAMMAR, LOGICK nor any other of the said Sciences, can subsist without GEOMETRY; ergo, most Worthy and Honourable.

YOU ask me how this Science was Invented, My Answer is this: That before the Generall Deluge, which is commonly Called NOAH'S Flood, there was a Man called LAMECH, as you may read in IV Chapter of Genesis; who had two Wives, the One called ADA, the other ZILLA; By ADA, he begat two SONS, IABAL and IUBAL, by ZILLA, he had One SON called TUBALL and a Daughter called Naamah. These four Children found the beginning of all Crafts in the World: IABAL found GEOMETRY and he Divided Flocks of Sheep, He first built a House of Stone and Timber.

HIS Brother IUBAL found the ART of MUSICK. He was the Father of all such as Handle the Harp and Organ. TUBAL-CAIN was the Instructer of Every Artificer in Brass and Iron, And. the Daughter found out the ART of Weaving.

THESE Children knew well that GOD would take Vengeance for SIN either by Fire or Water; Wherefore they Wrote their SCIENCES that they had found in Two Pillars, that they might be found after NOAH'S Flood.

ONE of the Pillars was Marble, for that will not Burn with any Fire, And the other Stone was Laternes for that will not drown with any Water.OUR Intent next is to Tell you Truely, how and in What manner these STONES were found whereon these SCIENCES were Written. THE Great HERMES (surnamed TRISMAGISTUS, or three times Great) Being both King, Priest and Philosopher, (in EGYPT) He found One of them, and Lived in the Year of the World Two Thousand and Seventy Six, in the Reign of NINUS, and some think him to be Grandson to CUSH, which was Grandson to NOAH, he was the first that began to Leave off Astrology To Admire the other Wonders of Nature; He proved, there was but One GOD, Creator of all Things, He Divided the Day into Twelve Hours. He is also thought to be the first to divide the ZODIACK into Twelve SIGNES, He was to OSYRIS, King of EGYPT; And is said to have Invented Ordinary Anno Mundi Writing, and Hierogliphiks, the first Laws of the Egyptians; And Divers Sciences, and Taught them MDCCCX unto other Men. AND at the Building of Babilon Masonry was much made of; And the king of Babilon, the Mighty NIMROD, was a Mason himselfe, as it's reported by Antient Histories, And when the City of NINEVE, and Other Cities of the East, were to be Built, NIMROD the King of Babilon Sent thither Masons at the request of the King of NINIVE his Cousin, And when he sent them forth, He gave them a CHARGE in this Manner. THAT they should be true to one another, and Love truely together; And. that they should serve the Lord truely for their Pay, so, that their Master might have honour, and all that belong unto him, And Severall other Charges He gave them; And this was the First time that Ever any MASON had any Charge of his CRAFT. MOREOVER when ABRAHAM and SARAH his Wife, went into EGYPT, and there taught the Anno Mundi. Seven Sciences to the EGYPTIANS; He had a Worthy SCHOLLAR whose Name was MIXILVIII EUCLIDE, and He learned right well, and became a Great Master of the Seven Sciences; And in His Days, It Befell, That the Lords and the Estates of the Realm, had so many Sons; And they had no Competent Livelyhood.to find their Children. WHEREFORE they took Council together with the King of the Land, How they might find their Children Honestly as Gentlemen, But could find no Manner of Good way, And. then Did they Proclaime through all the Land, that if there were any Man, that could Inform them, that he should be well rewarded for his Travell, And that he should hold him well pleased.

AFTER this CRY was made; then came the worthy CLARK EUCLYDE, and said to the King and the LORDS. IF YEA will Give me Your Children to Govern, I will Teach them One of the Seven SCIENCES, whereby they may live Honestly, as Gentlemen should; Under Condition, that Yea will Grant them, and That I may have Power to Rule them after the manner that science ought to be Ruled. And that the King and the Councell Grant Anon and seal his Commission. And then this Worthy Clark EUCLIDE took to him these Lord's Sons, and taught them the SCIENCE of GEOMETRY, in Practick, for the Work in STONE, all manner worthy Work, that belongeth to Building of CHURCHES, TEMPLES, TOWERS, CASTLES; And all other manner of Buildings; And He gave them a. Charge in this Manner. FIRST that they should be true to the King and to the Lord, that they Serve; and To the Fellowship whereof they are Admitted; And that they should Love and be true to one another; And that they should Call Each other his Fellow, or Else BROTHER; and not his Servant Knave, nor no other soul Name; And that they should truely deserve their Pay of the Lord; Or the Master of the Work, that they Serve.

THAT they should Ordain the Wisest of them to be the MASTER of the Work; And neither for Love nor Lynage, Riches nor Favour, to Sett another, that hath but little Cunning, to be Master of the Lord's Work; whereby the Lord should be Evil Served, and they Ashamed; And Also, that they should Call the Governour of the Work MASTER in the time that they work with him. AND many other Charges He gave them, that are too long to tell, And to all these Charges He made them Swear a great Oath, that Men Used at that time. AND He Ordain'd for them, a reasonable Pay, whereby they may live honestly; And Also that they should come and Assemble together every Year Once, to consult how they might Work best to serve the LORD, for his profit, And to their Own Credit, And. to Correct within themselves, him that had trespassed against the CRAFT. AND thus was the Craft Grounded there, And that WORTHY Crarft EUCLEDE Gave it the Name of GEOMETRY; And now It's call'd through all the LAND MASONRY SITHENSE Anno Mundi SITHENCE Long time after when the Children of ISRAEL were come into the Land of the MMCCCCLXXIV IEBUSITES which is now call'd IERUSALEM King DAVID began the Temple, that is called (TEMPLUM DOMINI) with the TEMPLE of IERUSALEM, alias the TEMPLE of the LORD. THE same king DAVID Loved MASONS and Cherished them, and gave them Good Pay. And he gave them the Charges in manner as they were given in EGYPT, by EUCLYDE; and other Charges more, as you shall Hear afterwards.

AFTER the decease of King DAVID SOLOMON sent to HIRAM, King of TYRE for one who was a Cunning Workman (called. HIRAM ABIF) the Son of a woman of the Line of Naphtali and of Urias the Israelite.

SOLOMON to HIRAM the King

KNOW thou that my Father having a will to Build a Temple to God, Hath been withdrawn from the Performance thereof by the Continual warrs and Troubles he hath had; for he never took rest, before he Either defeated his Enemies, or made them tributaries unto him FOR mine own part. I thank GOD for the peace which I possess; And for that, by the means thereof , I have opportunity (according to mine Own desire) to Build a Temple unto GOD; for he it is that Foretold my Father, that his House should be builded during my Reigne, FOR which Cause, I Pray you ,fend me some one of your Skilfullest men with my Servants to the wood Libanon, to hew down trees in that place; for the MACEDONIANS are more skilfull in Hewing and preparing Timber, than our People are, And I will pay the Cleavers of wood according to your Direction.

HIRAM unto KING SOLOMON

THOU hast Cause to thank GOD; in thou he had delivered thy Father's Kingdom into thy hands; TO thee I say, who art a Man, wife & full of Vertue; for which cause, since no news can come unto me more gracious, nor Office of Love more esteemed than this, I will accomplish all that thou requestest for after I have caused a great quantity of Ceadar & Cyprus wood to be cut down, I will send it thee by sea, by my servants; whom I will command (and furnish with Convenient Vessells of Burthen) to the end they may deliver the same in what place of thy kingdome it shall best please thee; that afterwards, thy Subjects may transport them to Jerusalem. YOU shall provide to furnish us with CORNE, whereof we stand in need, because we Inhabit an Island. SOLOMON King David's SON to finish the TEMPLE that his Father had begun, sent for MASONS into divers Countries, and gathered them togather, so that he had Fourscore thousand Workmen that were workers of STONE, and were all named MASONS, and he chose three THOUSAND of them to be Masters & Governours of his work. First of Kings VII XIV AND HIRAM King of Tyre sent his servants unto SOLOMON, for he was ever a Lover of King. David, And he sent Solomon Timber and workmen to help forward the Building of the Temple, And he sent one that was Named HIRAM ABIF a widows Son of the Line of Nephtali. He was a Master of Geometry, and was of all his Masons, Carvers, Ingravers and workmen, and Casters of Brass and all other Metalls that were used about the Temple. KING SOLOMON confirmed both the Charges and manners, that his Father had given to MASONS, thus was the worthy work of MASONRY Confirmed in Jerusalem, and many other Kingdoms, And he finished the Temple Anno Mundi M MM. CURIOUS Craftsmen walked about full wide in divers Countries; some to Learn more Craft and Cunning, others to teach them that had but little Cunning. AND at the Destruction of the FIRST Temple THE SECOND Temple began in the Reign of SYRUS LXX Years after the Destruction, it being hindred; It was XLVI Years in Building and was finished in Darius his Reign. MMMDXXII IN the Reign of Ptolmie and Cleopatra, ONIAS built a Jewish Temple in the place Called MMMDCCCXIII Bubastiss, and Called after his own Name. THE Tower of Straton (alias Ceasaria built by HEROD in Palestine and many other Curious works of Marble, As the Temple of Ceasar Agrippa to his Memory, in the Country called MMMDCCCXLII Zenodoras near to a place called Panion. He also pulled down the second Temple, that was finished in DARIUS his reign, and appointed one Thousand Carriages to draw stone to the place; And chose out Ten Thousand MMMDCCCCXLVI Cunning and expert workmen, to hew, and mould Stone; And. One Thousand he chose out and Cloathed, and made them Masters and Rulers of the work; And Anno Mundi built MMMDCCCCXLVII built a New Temple on the Foundation, which SOLOMON had laid, not inferior to the first. And was finished Nine years before the birth of our SAVIOR. MMMDCCCCLVI AFTER the birth of our Saviour, Aururiagus being King of Britain, Qaudius the Emperor came over with an Army; and fearing to be overthrown made a League with him; and gave him his Daughter in marriage; and that he should hold his Kingdom of Romans, and for the Emperor then returned. IN the Year XLIII, after the birth of CHRIST, MASONS came into England,

and built a Anno Christi XLIII goodly Monastry Near unto Glassenbury, with many CASTLE S and TOWERS.

    THIS sumptious Art of GEOMETRY; it being prosest by Emperors, Kings, Popes, Cardinals and Princes innumerable, who have all of them left us the Permanient Monuments of it in their several Anno Christi CXVII places of their Dominions; Nor will this I presume be denyed, when well considered ,that Renowned Example the TRAJAN COLLUM; it being one of the most superb Remainders of the Romans Magnificence, to be now seen Standing; And which has more Immortal lised the Emperor TRAJAN, than all the PENS of Hiftorians it was Erected to him, by the Senate and People of' Rome; In memory of those Great services he had rendred the Country, and to the end, the memory of it might remain to all succeeding Ages; and continue so long as the very Empire itselfe. Anno Christi CCC AND in Saint ALBANES time; the King of England that was a Pagan, Did wall the Town that was called Verulum; And Saint ALBAN was a worthy Knight, and Steward of the Kings Houshold; and had got the Government of the Realm, and also the Town walls, and Loved Masons well and cherished them much, and he made their Pay Right good, standing as the Realm then did; for he gave them two Shillings per week, and three pence to their Chear; For before that time through all the Land, a MASON had but a Penny a day and his meat, untill Saint ALBAN mended it. AND he got them a CHARTER of the King for to hold a Councell Yearly, and gave it the Name of an Assembly; and was thereat himselfe, and helped to make MASON, and gave them charges as yea. shall have afterwards. IT happened presently after the Martyrdom of St Alban, who is truly termed England's Proto Martyr; that a Certain King Invaded the Land and destroyed most of the Natives by Fire and sword That the SCIENCES of Masonry was much decayed, untill the Reign of Anno Domini DXCVI ETHELBERT King of Kent, Gregory the First Surnamed Magnus, sent into the Isle of Britaine a Monk with other Learned Men, to Preach the Christian Faith, for this Nation as yet, had not fully received it. this said Ethelbert, built a Church in Canterbury and Dedicated it to St Peter, and St Paul; and is supposed to have built, or restored the Church of St.Pauls in London: he also built the Church of St. Andrews in Rochester.

SIBERT King of the East Saxons by perswasions Of ATHELBERT King of Kent, having received, Anno Domini DCXXX the Christian faith; built the Monastry at Westminster, to the Honour of God, and St Peter. DCCCXCV SIGEBERT King of the East Angles began to Erect the University of Cambridge. ATHELSTANE began his Reign he was a Man beloved of all Men, he had great devotion towards the Churches, as appeared in the Building, adorning and. Endowing of Monasterys. He built one at Wilton in the Diocess of Salisbury; another at Michelney in Somersetshire: besides these; there were few famous Monasteries in this Realm, but that he adorned the fame, either with some new piece of Building, Iewells or Portions of Lands he greatly Enriched the Church of York. EDWIN Brother to King Athelstane Loved MASONS much more than his Brother did, and was a great Practizer of GEOMETRY and drew himselfe to Commune and talk with MASONS, to Learn the CRAFT, and afterward for the Love that Anno Domini DCCCCXXXII he had to MASONS and to the CRAFT. He was made a Mason, and got of his Brother a CHARTER, and Commission, to hold an Assembly himselfe at York; where they would within the Realm once a Year; to correct within themselves, faults and trespasses, that were done within the CRAFT, and he held an Assembly himselfe at YORK, and there made MASONS and gave them Charges, and taught the manner; and Commanded that Rule to be kept for ever after; and gave them the CHARTER, AND COMMISSION to keep; and made an Ordinance that it should be renewed from King to King. AND when the Assembly was gathered together, he made a CRY, that all Old MASONS, and young, that had any writing or understanding of the Charges, and manners. that were made before in the Land, or in any other; they should bring and shew them AND it was proved there were found some in French, some in Greek, some in English, and some in other Languages; and they were all to one Intent and purpose; and he made a Book thereof, how the Craft was founded; and he himselfe commanded, that it should. be read or told, when any MASON should be made, and for to give him his Charges; And from that Day untill this time, manners of MASONS have been kept in that form, as well as men might govern it. FURTHERMORE at divers Assemblys certain Charges have been made and ordained, by the best advice of Masters and FELLOWS.

EVERY Man that is a Mason, take right good heed. to these Charges. And if any man find himselfe Guilty in any of these Charges, he ought TO Amend, and pray to GOD, for his grace; especially you that are to be Charged.

Take good heed that yea may keep THE FIRST CHARGE IS THIS, That yea be true Men to God, and the HOLY CHURCH.

SECOND, THAT yea Use no HERESY, wilful; or run into Innovations, but be yea wise Men, and discreet in Every thing.

THIRD; That yea be not disloyall; nor Confederates in treasonable plotts; But if yea hear of any treachery against the Government, yea ought to discover it if yea cannot otherwise prevent it.

FOURTH; That yea be true to one another, (that is to say) to Every MASON of the Craft of MAS ONRY, that be MASONS allowed, yea shall do to them, as yea would they should doe unto you.

FIFTH; that yea keep all the Councell of your Fellows truly, be it in Lodge or in Chamber, And all other Councells that ought to be kept, by the way of Brotherhood.

SIXTH; that no Mason shall be a thief, or Conceal any such unjust Action, so far forth as he may wit or know.

SEVENTH, that every Allowed Mason shall be true to the Lord or Master whom he ferves, and shall serve him faithfully to his Advantage.

EIGHTH; that yea shall Call such Mason your Fellow or Brother, neither shall you use to him any scurilous Language.

NINTH; that yea shall not desire any unlawfull Communication with your fellows Wife, nor cast a wanton Eye upon his Daughter; with desire to defile her; nor his Maid servant or any wife put him to diswdship.

TENTH; that you Pay truly and honestly for your Meat and Drink wherever you Board; that the craft be not Slandered thereby. THESE be the Charges in General that BELONGS to Every free Mason to be kept, both by MASTERS and Fellows REHEARSE I will other Charges in singuler FOR MASTERS and Fellows

FIRST, That no Masters or Fellows shall take upon him any Lord's work nor any other Man's work unless he know himself Able and sufficient to perforrne the same, so that the Craft have no standard, nor disworship thereby, but the Lord may be well and truly served.

SECOND, that no Master take no work, but that he take it reasonably, fo that the Lord may be well served, and the Master get Sufficiently, to live handsomly and honestly, and to pay his Fellows truely their pay, as the manner is.

THIRD, that no Master nor Fellow shall supplant any other of their work, (that is to say) if another hath taken workein hand, or stand Master for any Lord's work; he shall not deale under hand, to mischiefe or undermine him, to put him out, Except he be unable of Cunning, to perform the work.

FOURTH, that no Master nor Fellow shall take any Apprentice but for the full term of seven Years; And that the Apprentice be Able of Birth (that is to say) free borne, and whole of Limbs, as a Man ought to be.

FIFTH, that no Master nor Fellow, take any Allowance or bribe of any Man, that is to be made a Mason, without the Assent, Consent, and Councell of his Fellows; and that he, that is to be made a MASON, be able in all manner of degrees (that is to say) freeborne; Come of good kindred, true, and no Bondman, and that he have his Right Limbs, as a Man ought to have.

SIXTH ,That no Master nor Fellow take an Apprentice unless he hath sufficient Occupation to set him at work Nay to set three of his Fellows; or two at least at work.

SEVENTH, That no Master or Fellow shall take no Mans work to Task, that Used, or was wont to Journey work.

EIGHTH, That Every Master shall give pay to his Fellow according as they deserve so that he be not deceived by false workmen.

NINETH, That no Man slander another behind his back to make him loose his good Name, and thereby also make him suffer in his way of Living.

TENTH, That no Fellow within the Lodge, or without; Misanswer, or give another reproachfull Language, without some reasonable Cause.

ELEVENTH, That every Mason shall Reverence his Elder; and put him in workship.

TWELFTH, That no Mason shall be a Common player at Hazard, or at Dice, or at Cards nor any other unlawfull Game whereby the Craft might be slandered.

THIRTEENTH, That no Mason shall be a Common Leecher, nor Pander, or Baud whereby the Craft might be slandered.

FOURTEENTH, That no Fellow go into the City or Town in Night time, without he hath some one or other with him to BEAR Witness that he was in honest places.

FIFTEENTH, That Every Master and Fellow, shall come to the Assembly, if that be within Fifty Miles about him, if he hath any warning, And if he hath Trespassed against the Craft, then abide the Award of the Masters and Fellows, and make satisfaction accordingly, if they are able; But if not Submit to their reasonable Award; Then they shall go to Common Law.

SIXTEENTH, That no Master or Fellow make any Mould or Square, or Rule to Mould Stones withall; but such as are allowed by the Fraternity.

SEVENTEENTH, That Every Mason shall Receive and Cherish strange Fellows, when they Come over the Country, and set them at work if they will as the manner is (that is to say) if he hath Mould Stones in his place, or else he shall refresh him with money to Carry him to the next Lodge.

EIGHTEENTH, That every Mason shall truely serve the LORD for his pay; And every Master shall truely make an END of his Work; be it Talk or Journey If he have his Demand, and all he ought to have. THESE Charges That we have now Rehearsed unto you and all other that belong to MASONS YEA shall keep.

SO Help you GOD, and the ITALLIDOM

Finis

Thomas Tew Manuscript
The Book of Masons
circa 1680

Good Brethren and fellows. My purpose is to show you how and in what sort of manner this Worthy Craft of Masonry was first founded and afterwards how it was and so maintained & upholden by worthy Kings and Princes and many of the worshipfull men. And also them that so true were with Ponderasion. Unto you the charges that belongeth to Every Free Mason to keep. For it is a Science that is worthy to be kept for a working craft and Virtuous Science, For it is one of the Seven Liberal Sciences and then be the name of them. First is Grammer that teacheth a man to speak and write truly. The Second is Rhetorick that teacheth a man to speak in Subtel terms. The third is Dilectick That teacheth a man to discern to know truth and Falshood asunder. The Fourth- Arithmetick that teacheth to Reckon and count all manner of numbers. The fifth is Geometra and it teacheth us Mete and Measure the Earth and other things of the which is Masonry; The sixth Science is Musick that teacheth the Craft of Song and voice of tongue Organ and harp. The Seventh is called Astronomy and teacheth to know the Course of the Sunn and of the Starrs. These be the Seven Liberal Sciences the which be all found by one Science which is called Geomtry. This may you prove that all the Sciences in the World were grounded upon this science-Geometry for it teacheth Mete Measure Ponderasion & Weight of all manner of kind of measure, And there is no man that Worketh any kind of Craft but Worketh by Measure, Nor any man that buyeth & Selleth but useth the Measure or Weight & that belongeth to Geometry and these Craft do find all other of the Six Sciences & especially the Plowman and Tillers of all kind of Graine Corn Seeds Vines Planters and Sellers of Fruit, nor cannot Plow Till sow or sett without Geometry. For Grammer nor Astronomy nor any of all these Sciences Cannot find a man one measure or Mete without Geomtry. Wherefore that Science may well be called the Most Worthiest science of all Sciences which can find be the Mete and Measure to the Rest. If you ask how this Worthy Science was begun, I shall tell you, Before the flood of Noah there was a man that was Called Cain the Sower. Cain killed his

Brother Abel With an Arrow as the Scriptures so sayeth In the fourth chapter of Genesis: Thus Cain begat Enoch and unto Enoch was Born Jarid.

Edinburgh Register House Manuscript
Some Questions that Masons use to Put Those Who have Ye Word Before they will Acknowledge them
circa 1696

Quest. 1 Are you a mason.
Answer: yes

Q: 2 How shall I know it?
Ans: you shall know it in time and place convenient.

Remark the forsaid answer is only to be made when there is company present who are not masons. But if there be no such company by, you should answer by signes tokens and other points of entrie

Q: 3 What is your first point?
Ans: Tell me the first point ile tell you the second, The first is to heill and conceall, second, under no less pain, which is then cutting of your throat, For you most make that sign, when you say that

Q: 4 Where wes you entered?
An: At the honourable lodge.

Q:5 What makes a true and perfect lodge?
An: Seven masters, five entered apprentices, A dayes journey from a burroughs town without bark of dog or crow of cock

Q: 6 Does no less make a true and perfect lodge,
An: yes five masons and three entered apprentices &c.

Q: 7 Does no less.
An: The more the merrier the fewer the better chear

Q: 8 What is the name of your lodge
An: Kilwinning

Q: 9 How stands your lodge
An: east and west as the temple of Jerusalem

Q: 10 Where wes the first lodge.
An: In the porch of Solomons Temple

Q: 11 Are there any lights in your lodge
An: yes three the north east. s w, and eastern passage The one denotes the master mason, the other the warden The third the setter croft.

Q: 12 Are there any jewells in your lodge
An: Yes three, Perpend Esler a Square pavement and a broad oval

Q: 13 where shall I find the key of your lodge?
Ans: Three foot and an half from the lodge door under a perpend esler, and a green divot. But under the lap of my liver where all my secrets of my heart lie

Q: 14 Which is the key of your lodge
Ans: a weel hung tongue

Q: 15 where lies the key
Ans: In the bone box

After the masons have examined you by all or some of these Questions and that you have answered them exactly and mad the signes, they will acknowledge you, but not a master mason or fellow croft but only as [? = an] apprentice, soe they will say I see you have been in the Kitchine but I know not if you have been in the hall, Ans I have been in the hall as weel as in the kitchine

Quest 1 Are you a fellow craft
Ans: yes

Quest 2 How many points of the fellowship are ther

Ans: fyve viz foot to foot Knee to Kn[ee] Heart to Heart, Hand to Hand and ear to ear. Then make the sign of fellowship and shake hand and you will be acknowledged a true mason. The words are in the I of the Kings Ch 7, 21, and in 2 chr: ch 3 verse last.

The Forme of Giveing the Mason Word

Imprimis you are to take the person to take the word upon his knees and after a great many ceremonies to frighten him you make him take up the bible and laying his right hand on it you are to conjure him, to sec[r]ecie, By threatning that if [he] shall break his oath the sun in the firmament will be a witness agst him and all the company then present, which will be an occasion of his damnation and that likewise the masons will be sure to murder him, Then after he has promised secrecie They give him the oath a[s] follows

By God himself and you shall answer to god when you shall stand nakd before him, at the great day, you shall not reveal any pairt of what you shall hear or see at this time whither by word nor write nor put it in wryte at any time nor draw it with the point of a sword, or any other instrument upon the snow or sand, nor shall you speak of it but with an entered mason, so help you god.

After he hes taken the oath he is removed out of the company, with the youngest mason, where after he is sufficiently frighted with 1000 ridicolous postures and grimmaces, He is to learn from the sd mason the manner of makeing his due guard whis [? = which] is the signe and the postures and words of his entrie which are as follows ffirst when he enters again into the company he must make a ridiculous bow, then the signe and say God bless the honourable company. Then putting off his hat after a very foolish manner only to be demonstrated then (as the rest of the signes are likewise) he says the words of his entrie which are as follows Here come I the youngest and last entered apprentice As I am sworn by God and St John by the Square and compass, and common judge to attend my masters service at the honourable lodge, from munday in the morning till saturday at night and to keep the Keyes thereof, under no less pain then haveing my tongue cut out under my chin

Edinburgh Register House Manuscript

and of being buried, within the flood mark where no man shall know, then he makes the sign again and with drawing his hand under his chin alongst his throat which denotes that it be cut out in caise he break his word.

Then all the mason present whisper amongst themselves the word beginning at the youngest till it comes to the master mason who gives the word to the entered apprentice.

Now it is to be remarked that all the signes and words as yet spoken of are only what belong to the entered apprentice, But to be a master mason or fellow craft there is more to be done which after follows.

First all the prentices are to be removed out of the company and none suffered to stay but matters.

Then he who is to be admitted a member of fellowship is putt again to his knees, and gets the oat[h] administrated to him of new afterwards he must go out of the company with the youngest mason to learn the postures and signes of fellowship, then comeing in again, He makes the masters sign, and sayes the same words of entrie as the app[rent]ice did only leaving out the com[m]on Judge then the masons whisper the word among themselves beginning at the youngest as formerly afterwards the youngest mason must advance and put himself into the posture he is to receive the word and sayes to the eldest mason in whispering ***

The worthy masters and honourable company greet you weel, greet you weel, greet you weel.

Then the master gives him the word and gripes his hand after the masons way, which is all that is to be done to make him a perfect mason.

Sloane Ms. No. 3329
circa 1700

A narrative of the Freemasons word and signes.

First they discover other by signes next they go in private to discourse, one signe is by giving their right hand a cast cross their brest from left to right with the tops of their Fingers about 3 or 4 inches below their chin, another is by puling of their hat wth their right hand their two first fingers above and the thumb and all the rest below the hats brim puling it of and giving it a cast from Left to right then on their head another is of drinking giving the glass a acast cross under their chin from left to right: another is taking their handke^r by the corner wth their right hand and throw it over their Left should^r letting it hang down their back and so walk a few steps along if any mason see it they will follow and take him by the hand; their gripe for fellow craftes is grasping their right hands in Each other thrusting their thumb naile close upon the third Joynt of each oth^{rs} first finge^r their Masters gripe is grasping their right hands in each othe^r placing their four finger's nails hard upon the Carpus or end of others wrists and their thumb nailes thrust hard directly between the second Joynt of the thumb and the third Joynt of the first Fing^r but some say the mast^{rs} grip is the same I last discribed only each of their midle Fing^r must reach an inch or three barly cornes Length higher to touch upon a vein y^t comes from the heart. Anoth^r signe is placing their right heell to the inside of their left in forme of a square so walk a few steps backward and forward and at every third step make a Little stand placeing their feet Square as afores^d this done if any masons *p*ceive it they will presently come to you if you come where any masons tooles lyes lay y^m in forme of a square *they will presently know y^t a free brother hath been there or a free broth^r coming where free masons are at worke if he takes some of their tooles & lay y^m in form of a square* it is a signe to discover him, or if he takes one of their tooles or his own staff and strike saftly on the wall or worke saying this is bose or hollow if their be any free broth^r at the work he will answ^r it is solid wch words are signes to discov^r each oth^r. Anoth^r signe some use bending their right arme in form of a Square & laying the palm of their left hand upon their heart. Anoth^r is by hoisting their eyes toward the east and twisting their mouth toward ye west. Anoth^r is bending their right knee holding up their hand towards the east and if it be night or dark they will give two little haughts and a great one as if they were forceing a bone or a lump out of their throat, they will say ye day is for seeing the night for hereing. Anoth^r signe is by lending you a crooked pin or a bit of pap^r cut in the forme of a square on receipt of wch you must come from w^t place or company soever you are in by virtue of your oath and by ye aforementioned sign of ye hat or hand you are to come if it were from the top of a Steeple to know their pleasure and to assist them And to lett you know he wants money he will hold a bitt of a pipe (or some such thing) to you saying can you change a cole pence if you have money you say is if you have none say no, some will signifye their want of money by pulling their knife out of the sheath and giving it to a broth^r in company or alone if the broth^r have money he takes the knife puting it in it's sheath and returne it, if he have none he will return it bare as he reced it: which many of them do notwithstanding their oath and many oth^r signes they reject thô by oath they are bound to obey all; Another signe is by taking their handk^r in their right hand and blow their nose then holding it straight out before them they give it two Little shakes and a big one. Anoth^r signe is knocking at any door two little knocks and the third a big one. They have anoth^r signe used at the Table drinking when the glass goes not fast enough round they say star the guile.

To Discourse a mason in France, Spaine, or Turkey (say they) the signe is to kneel Down on his left knee and hold up his right hand to the sunn and the outlandish Broth^r will presently take him up but beleive me if they go on their knees on that acco^t they may remain there; or any persons observe their signes as Long as ye Jews will remaine on their beliefe to rece. their wished for Mesias from the East.

Here followeth there private discourse by way of Question and Answer.

(Question.) Are you a mason.
(Answ^r.) Yes I am a freemason.

(Q.) How shall I know that.
(A.) By perfect signes and tokens and the first poynts of my enterance.

(Q.) Which is the first signe or token shew me the first and I will shew you the second.
(A.) The first is heal and conceal or conceal and keep secrett by no less paine than cutting my tongue from my throat.

(Q.) Where were you made a Mason.
(A.) In a just and perfect or just and Lawfull Lodge.

(Q.) What is a just and perfect or just and Lawfull Lodge.
(A.) A just and perfect Lodge is two Interprintices two fellow craftes and two Mast^{rs} more or fewer the more the merrier the fewer the bett^r chear but if need require five will serve that is two Interprintices two fellow Craftes and one Mast^r on the highest hill or Lowest Valley of the World without the crow of a Cock or the bark of a Dogg.

(Q.) From whome do you derive your principalls.
(A.) From a great^r than you.

(Q.) Who is that on earth that is great^r than a freemason.
(A.) He y^t was caryed to ye highest pinnicall of the Temple of Jerusalem.

(Q.) Whith^r is your Lodge shut or open.
(A.) It is shut.

(Q.) Where Lyes the Keys of the Lodge doore.
(A.) They Ley in a bound Case or und^r a three cornerd pavem^t about a foot and halfe from the Lodge door.

(Q.) W^t is the Keys of your Lodge Doore made of.
(A.) It is not made of Wood, Stone, Iron, or Steel or any sort of mettle but the tongue of a good report behind a Broth^{rs} back as well as before his face.

(Q.) How many Jewles belong to your Lodge.

(A.) There are three the Square pavem^t the blazing Star and the Danty tassley.

(Q.) How Long is the Cable rope of your Lodge.
(A.) As Long as from the Lop of the Liver to the root of the tongue.

(Q.) How many Lights are in your Lodge.
(A.) Three the sun the mast^r and the Square.

(Q.) How high is your Lodge.
(A.) Without foots yards or Inches it reaches to heaven.

(Q.) How Stood your Lodge.
(A.) East and west as all holly Temples Stand.

(Q.) W^{ch} is the mast^{rs} place in the Lodge.
(A.) The east place is the Mast^{rs} place in the Lodge and the Jewell resteth on him first and he setteth men to works w^t the Mast^{rs} have in the foornoon the wardens reap in the Afternoon.

In some places they discourse as followeth (Viz^t)

(Q.) Where was the word first given.
(A.) At the Tower of Babylon.

(Q.) Where did they first call their Lodge.
(A.) At the holy Chapell of St John.

(Q.) How Stood your Lodge.
(A.) As the said holy Chapell and all other holy Temples stand (viz.) east and west.

(Q.) How many lights are in your Lodge.
(A.) Two one to see to go in and another to see to work.

(Q.) What were you sworne by.
(A.) By god and the Square.

(Q.) Whither above the Cloathes or und^r the C[loathes].
(A.) Und^r the Cloathes.

(Q.) Under what Arme.
(A.) Und^r the right Arme.

God is Gratfull to all Worshipfull Mast^{rs} and fellows in that Worshipfull Lodge from whence we last came and to you good fellow w^t is your name.
A. - J or B. then giving the grip of the hand he will say Broth^r John greet you well you.
A. - Goe good greeting to you dear Broth^r.

Another salutation is giving the mast^{rs} or fellows grip saying the right worshipfull the mast^{rs} and fellows in that worshipfull Lodge from whence we Last came greet you greet you greet you well, then he will repley Gods good greeting to you dear Brother.
Anoth^r they haue called the mast^{rs} word and is Mahabyn which is allways divided into two words and standing close with their Breasts to each oth^r the inside of Each oth^{rs} right Ancle joynts the Mast^{rs} grip by their right hands and the top of their Left hand fingers thurst close on ye small of each oth^{rs} Backbone and in that posture they stand till they whisp^r in each oth^{rs} eares ye one Maha- the oth^r repleys Byn.

The Oath

The mason word and every thing therein contained you shall keep secrett you shall never put it in writing directly or Indirectly you shall keep all that we or your attend^{rs} shall bid you keep secret from Man Woman or Child Stock or Stone and never reveal it but to a brother or in a Lodge of Freemasons and truly observe the Charges in ye Constitucion all this you promise and swere faithfully to keep and observe without any manner of Equivocation or mentall resarvation directly or Indirectly so help you god and by the Contents of this book.

So he kisses the Book &c.

The Kevan Manuscript
The Form of Giving the Mason Word
circa 1714-1720

The Person qo is to geet ye word is put upon his knees, & after a grate many Serimonys to frighten him they make him take up the Bible & Laying his right hand upon it, they Conjure him by Severall thretings yt if he shall brake his Oath; The Sun in ye Firmament & all ye Company there present will be witnesses agt him qh will be ye occasione of his Damnatione & yt Likewise they'l be sure to Murder him : Then after he has sworne secrsie they wille give him the Oath as Follows .'.

By : God himselfe & as you shall answer to God qh you shall Stand naked befor him a ye grate day of Judgment .'. you shall not reveall any poynt of what you shall see or hear at this time neither by word or writing at any time or .'. draw it wt ye poynt of a Sword or any other instrument upon ye Snow, or Sand, Nor shall you Speake of it but wt .'. an Entered Measone . . So hele me God .'. After he has taken the oath he is removed out of ye Company wt ye yowngast Masone, where after he is Suffieintly frightn .'. ed wt a thousand Grimasses & posturs He is to Learn from ye Sd Mason ye manner of Making [the due guard] which is the Signs and Posturs (Signs Postures and words] of .'. his [entry] qh are a follow Here come I ye youngast & Last Entered prentise, as I am sworne by God & St. John by ye Square & Campass .'. & common Judge to attend my Mrs : service at ye Honourable Lodge from Munday Morning till Setturdays night to keep ye Keys thereof under no Less paine then to have my tounge cut out under my Chinn & to be buryed wtin ye flood marke wher .'. no man shall know .'. Then he makes ye Signe again qh is by Drawing his hand under his Chin alonge his throate qh denotes it is to be Cut in case he broke his worde Then all yy Masons present whisper the word amongst emselves beginning [at the youngest] till it .'. come to ye Mr Masone, qo gives ye worde to the entered Prentise .'.

Now it is to be Marked yt all ye Signs & words as yet spoken off are only qt belongs to Entered prentises but to [be] a Mr : .'. Masone or fellow craft [there is more to be done as after follows] : First all ye Prentices are to be removed out of the Company & none Suffered to stay by only .'. Mrs : Then [he] qo is to be admitted a member of fellowship is put again to his knees & geets ye oath administered to him anew .'. Afterward he most go out of the Company wt ye youngast Mr to Learne the word & Signs of fellowship yn comming .'. inn again he makes ye Mr Signs of fellowship & says the same words of entry [as the apprentice did] only keeping out ye Coming [Common] Judge (i.e. a gauge or template used as a guide in cutting stones; in Jamieson's Scottish Dictionary, a Jedge is a gauge or standard.) yn ye Mrs .'. whisper the word among emselves beginning at ye youngest as befor, Afterwards ye younge masone advancess & puts him selfe in a posture wherein he is to receive ye word & says to them : The Honourable company ye worthy Masons & .'. honourable company yt I come from Greet you well, Greet you well, Greete you well .'. [Then the master {Mason} gives him the word and gripes his hand after the masons way which is all that is to be done to make him a perfect mason. - Edinburgh Register House MS.] Some Questions that Masons use to put to these who profess to have ye Mason word before they wille Acknowlagde them .'.

1. Are you a Mason
Yes endeed I am .'.

2. How shall I know that
In time and place convenient Not[e] : This answer isonly to be made when there .'. are company present qo are not masons, Bot if there be no such company by you you should answer, by Signs & .'. tokens & other poynts of Entry .'.

3. What is the first poynt of Entry?
tell me the first & I'l tell thee the seacond : The first is tohear & Conseal .'. The Second under no Hell [less] pain (Drawing the right Hand from the Left ear to the right) yn Cutting yr Throat, [for you must make that sign when you say that] .'.

The Kevan Manuscript

4. Where way you Entred?
Att Honowrable Lodge .'.

5. What makes a true & perfect Lodge?
7 : Mrs : 5 Prenices & a days Jurny from a Burrowghs toun wtout .'. barke of Doge or crow of Cocke .'.

6. Doeth no less make a true & Perfect lodge?
4 Mrs 3 entered Prentices & ye rest as befor [the Edingurgh text says : ". . . five masons and three entered apprentices &c."] .'.

7. Dose no Less?
The Mo the Mirryer & ye fewer the better Chear .'.

8. What is the name of your Lodge
The Lodge of Killewinning .'.

9. How Stands you Lodge?
Easte & west as the Temple of Jerusalem .'.

10. Where was the first Lodge?
In the Porch of Sollomons Temple.'.

11. Are there Lights in your Lodge?
Three, ye North East, Southwest, & Easters [Eastern] passages ye first .'. denots the Mr Masone, the Second the word {Words - Chetwode] [warden - Edinburgh] the third the fellowcraft [ffellow-Craft - Chetwode] {setter croft - Edinburgh] .'.

12. Are there any Jewels in you Lodge?
Three, a Perpendester [Perpend-ashlar] a Square Pavement & a covered Kinall [broked-mall - Chetwode - probably correct; i.e. a heavy maul for striking the chisel when the face of a stone in 'broached' i.e. indented or furrowed] [Broad ovall - Edinburgh] .'.

13. Where Shall I find the Key of you Lodge?
Three foot & an Half from the Lodge door under a .'. Perpendaster [Perpend-ashlar] [and a] Green Divot .'.

14. What do you mean by a Perpendester & green Divot?
I mean not noly under a Perpendester I green .'. Divot, but under the Lape of my Liver where all Secrets of my Hart Lie [Edinburgh makes one question of nos. 13 and 14.] .'.

15. Which is the Key of you Lodge ?
A well Hunge tounge .'.

16. Where Lys yt Key ?
In The Bone Box .'.

After The Masons have Examened You by all or Some of these Questions & yt .'. you Have answered em Exactly [and made the sign(s)] ; they will acknowladge you as a Prenticer .'. But not as a Mason or Fellow Craft .'.

17. So they will say We see you have been in the Kitchin but know not yt you have been in ye Hall
I have .'. been in the Hall as well as in the Kitchin .'.

18. Are you a Fellow Craft
Yes .'.

19. How many Poynts of Fellowship are there
5 : Viz: Foot to Foot, Knee to Knee, Harte to .'. Harte, Hand to Hand, & Ear to Eare, qh make the Signs of Fellowship ; & shake hands, & .'.

You wille be Acknowladged to be a true Masone .'. The Worde is in I : Kings 7 : 21 : & in 2d : Chron 3d : Last Varse the wholl .'. Varse but especially the words Jachin & Boaz.

Robert's Constitutions (1722)
The Old Constitutions
Belonging to the Ancient and Honourable Society of Free and Accepted Masons.

Taken from a Manuscript wrote above Five Hundred Years since.
London:
Printed and sold by J. Roberts, in *Warwick-Lane*, MDCCXXII.
(Price Six-Pence.)

The Preface

If any Thing could have escaped the Censures of this litigious Age; if the most innocent inoffensive Set of Men in the World could be free from Satyr and Sarcasm, one would have thought the Ancient and Noble Society of Free-Masons should have been the Men. What have they not to recommend them to the World, and gain the Favour and Protection of wise and honest Men?

As their Art is the most Ancient, so their Profession of it is most Honourable. The Necessity the World was early in of the Profession of a Mason, proves their Usefulness; for I believe it will not be doubted, that Men had Houses before they had Cloaths, as they had Altars before they had Temples. Cain built a City, and Abel, no doubt, built an Altar, when he offered his Sacrifice to the LORD.

THUS useful, and thus ancient, it cannot be wondered if the World honour'd them with all the Tokens of Respect, which in those Days they were capable of, and perhaps more than we have yet an Account of.

THESE Honours, and this Respect, it cannot be doubted brought Men of Value among them, who thought it not below them to wear the Badge of the Society, and to acknowledge themselves to be Favourers of their Greatness, as they were Lovers of Art.

UNDER the Protection of such Persons of Honour and Interest, it is not to be express'd what mighty Fabricks they have erected, what glorious Buildings they have rais'd, from the Temple of Solomon to the magnificent Pile of St. Peter's at Rome.

HOW this Society has been preserv'd; How regularly they have acted; on what wholesome Laws they have been founded, and how carefully they have observ'd and regarded those Laws, as the just Cement of the Society, that is partly to be seen in this Tract, and it will speak for itself.

NOR is their Value lessen'd or abated at all by the Dust and Scandal rais'd by any Men against them, or by the freedom they have taken to banter and rally them. The Dirt thrown at them flyes back on those that cast it, and the Honour of the Society of Free-Masons remains entire. So that none of the Persons of Honour who have lately grac'd the Society with their Presence, have yet seen any Reason to be asham'd of them, or to withdraw their Protection from them.

MUCH more might be said to their Honour, but the following Piece of Antiquity is sufficient, and will give every Reader an Authentick Account of them. It has yet seen the World but in Fragments, but is now put together as a Thing of too much Significancy to pass our Observation, and which will effectually vindicate the Ancient Society of Free-Masons from all that has or can be said against them.

The History of Free Masons, &c.

THE Almighty Father of Heaven, with the Wisdom of the Glorious Son, thro' the Goodness of the Holy Ghost, Three Persons in one Godhead, be with our Beginning, and give us his grace so to govern our Lives, that we may come to his Bliss, that never shall have end. Amen.

GOOD Brethren and Fellows, our Purpose is to tell you how, and in what manner the Craft of *Masonry* was begun, and afterwards how it was founded by worthy Kings and Princes, and other wise Men, hurtful to none, and also to them that be true, we will declare doth belong to every Free Mason to keep firm good Faith, if you take Heed thereunto it is well worthy to be kept, which is contain'd in the Seven Liberal Sciences as follows, viz.

Imprimis, It's *Grammar* that teaches a Man to speak truly, and write truly

II. - It's *Rhetorick* that teaches a Man to speak fair, and in subtle Terms.

III. - It's *Logick* that teaches a Man to discern truth from Falshood.

IV. - It's *Arithmetick* that teaches a Man to Accompt, and reckon all manner of Numbers.

V. - It's *Geometry* that teaches Mett and Measure of any Thing, and from thence cometh *Masonry*.

VI. - It's *Musick* that teacheth Song and Voice.

VII. - It's *Astronomy* which teacheth to know the Course of the Sun, Moon, and other Ornaments of Heaven.

Note, I pray you, That these Seven are contain'd under *Geometry*, for it teacheth Mett and Measure, Ponderation and Weight for every Thing in and upon the whole Earth for you to know; that every Craftsman works by Measure; He or she that buys or sells, is by Weight or Measure; Husbandmen, Navigators, Planters, and all of them, use *Geometry*; for neither *Grammar*, *Rhetorick*, *Logick*, nor any other of the said Sciences can subsist without *Geometry*, *ergo*, most worthy and honourable.

You ask me how this Science was invented; my Answer is this, That before the General Deluge, which is commonly called *Noah's* Flood, there was a Man called *Lamech*, as you may read in the Fourth Chapter of *Genesis*, who had two Wives, the one called *Ada*, the other *Zilla*; by *Ada* he begat two Sons, *Jabal* and *Jubal*; by *Zilla* he had one Son called *Tubal*, and a Daughter called *Naamah*. These four Children found the beginning of all Crafts in the World: *Jabal* found out *Geometry*, and he divided Flocks of Sheep, and Lands; he first built a House of Stone and Timber. *Jubal* found out *Musick*; *Tubal* found out the Smith's Trade or Craft, also of Gold, Silver, Copper, Iron and Steel; *Naamah* found out the Craft of Weaving.

And these children knew that GOD would take Vengeance for Sins, either by Fire or Water, wherefore they did write these Sciences, that they had found, on two Pillars of Stone, that they might be found after that GOD had taken Vengeance; the one was *Marble*, that would not burn, the other was *Latress*, that would not drown in Water; so that the one would be preserved, and not consumed, if GOD would any People should live upon the Earth.

It resteth now to tell you how these Stones were found, whereon the said Sciences were written, after the said Deluge: It so pleased God Almighty, that the Great *Hermarmes*, whose Son *Lunie* was, who was the son of Sem, who was the son of Noah. The said *Hermarmes* was afterwards called *Hermes*, the Father of *Lunie*, he found one of the two Pillars of Stone. He found these Sciences written thereon, and taught them to other Men. And at the Tower of *Babylon*, *Masonry* was much made on; for the King of *Babylon*, who was *Nemorth*, was a *Mason*, and serv'd the Science; and when the City of *Ninevah*, and other Cities of the *East*, should be built, *Nemorth* sent there threescore Masons, at the Desire of the King of *Ninevah*; and when they went forth, he gave them a Charge after this manner, That they should be true one to another, and love one another, that he might have Worship by them in sending them to his Cozen the King. He also gave them Charge concerning their Science; and then it was the first time that any *Mason* had Charge of his Work. Also *Abraham*, and *Sarah* his Wife, went into *Egypt*, and taught the *Egyptians* the Seven Liberal Sciences; and he had an ingenious Schollar called *Euclydes*, who perfectly learned the said Liberal Sciences.

It happen'd in his Days, the Lords and States of the Realm had so many Sons unlawfully begotten by other Men's Wives, that the Land was burthen'd with them, having small Means to maintain them withal; the King understanding thereof, caused a Parliament to be called or summoned for Redress, but being so Numberless that no Good could be done with them, he caused Proclamation to be made through the Realm, that if any Man could devise any Course how to maintain them, to inform the King, and he should be well rewarded; whereupon *Euclydes* came to the King, and said thus, My noble Sovereign, if I may have the Order of Government of those Lords' Sons, I will teach them the Seven Liberal Sciences, whereby they may live honestly like Gentlemen, provided that you will grant me Power over them by virtue of your Dominion; which was immediately effected, and there *Euclydes* gave them these Admonitions following

I. - To be true to their King.

II. -To be true to the Master they serve.

III. - To be true, and love one another.

IV. - Not to miscall one another, &c.

V. - To do their Work so duly, that they may deserve their Wages at their Master's Hands.

VI. - To ordain the wisest of them Master of the rest of the Work.

VII. - To have such reasonable Wages, that the Workman may live honestly, and with Credit.

VIII. - To come and assemble together in the Year, to take Council in their Craft how they may work best to serve their Lord and Master, for his Profit, and their own Credit, and to correct such as have offended.

Note, that *Masonry* was heretofore term'd *Geometry*, and sithence the Children of *Israel* came to the Land of *Bethest*, which is now called *Emens*, in the Country of *Jerusalem*, where they began a Temple, which is now called the Temple of *Jerusalem*: And King *David* loved *Masons* well and cherish'd them, for he gave them good Payment, and gave them a Charge, as *Euclydes* had given them before in *Egypt*, and further, as hereafter followeth; and after the Decease of King *David*, *Solomon* his Son finished the Temple that his Father had began; he sent for *Masons* of divers Nations, to the Number of Four and Twenty Thousand, of which Number Four Thousand were elected and created Masters and Governors of the Work. And there was a King of another Region or Country, called *Hiram*, who loved well King *Solomon*, and he gave him Timber for the Work; and he had a Son called *Amon*, and he was Master of *Geometry*, and he was chief Master of all his *Masons* of Carving-Work, and of all other Work of *Masonry* that belong'd to the Temple, as appears by the Bible in *Lib. Regum Cap. 4*. And King *Solomon* confirmed all Things concerning *Masons*, that *David* his Father had given in Charge; and then *Masons* did travel divers Countries, some to augment their Knowledge in the said Art, and to instruct others.

And it happen'd that a curious *Mason* named *Memongrecus*, that had been at the building of *Solomon's* Temple, came into *France*, and taught the Science of *Masonry* to the *Frenchmen*; and there was a King of *France* called *Carolus Martel*, who loved greatly *Masonry*, who sent for the said *Memongrecus*, and learned of him the said Sciences, and became one of the Fraternity; and thereupon began great Works, and liberally did pay his Workmen: He confirm'd unto them a large Charter, and was yearly present at their Assembly, which was a great Honour and Encouragement unto them; and thus came the Science into *France*.

The Knowledge of *Masonry* was unknown in *England* until St. *Alban* came thither, who instructed the King in the said Science of *Masonry*, and also in Divinity, who was a *Pagan*: He walled the Town now called St. *Alban*; he became in high Favour with the King, insomuch that he was Knighted, and made the King's Chief Steward, and the Realm was governed by him under the said King. He greatly cherished and loved *Masons*, and truly paid them their Wages Weekly, which was 3 *s*. 6 *d*. the Week. He also purchased for them a Charter from the King to hold a General Assembly and Council Yearly. He made many *Masons* and gave them such a Charge as is hereafter declared.

It happen'd presently after the Martyrdom of St. *Alban*, who is truly term'd *England's Proto-Martyr*, that a certain King invaded the Land, and destroy'd most of the Natives by Fire and Sword, that the Science of *Masonry* was much decay'd, until the Reign of King *Athelston*, which some write *Adleston*, who brought the Land to Peace and Rest, from the insulting *Danes*. He began to build many Abbies, Monasteries, and other Religious Houses, as also Castles and divers Fortresses for Defence of his Realm. He loved *Masons* more than his Father; he greatly study'd *Geometry*, and sent into many Lands for Men expert in the Science. He gave them a very large Charter, to hold a Yearly Assembly, and Power to correct Offenders in the said Science; and the King himself caused a General Assembly of all *Masons* in his Realm, at *York*, and there made many *Masons*, and gave them a deep Charge for Observation of all such Articles as belonged unto *Masonry*, and delivered them the said Charter to keep; and when this Assembly was gathered together, he caused a Cry to be made, that if any of them had any Writing that did concern *Masonry*, or could inform the King of any Thing or Matter that was wanting in the said Charge already delivered, that they or he should shew them to the King, or recite them to him; and there were some in *French*, some in *Greek*, and some in *English*, and other Languages, whereupon the King caused a Book to be made, which declared how the Science was first invented, and the Utility thereof, which Book he commanded to be read, and plainly declared, when any Man was to be made a *Mason* that he might fully understand what Articles, Rules and Orders he was obliged to observe; and from that time unto this Day *Masonry* hath been much respected and preserved, and divers new Articles have been added to the said Charge, by good Advice and Consent of the Masters and Fellows.

Tunc Unus ex Senioribus veniat librum illi qui Injurandum reddat & ponat Manum in libro vel supra librum dum Articulus & Precepta sibi legentur.

Saying thus by way of Exhortation,

MY loving and respected Friends and Brethren, I humbly beseech you, as you love your Soul's eternal Welfare, your Credit, and your Country's Good, to be very Careful in Observation of these Articles that I am about to read to this Deponent; for ye are obliged to perform them as well as he, so hoping of your Care herein, I will, by God's Grace, begin the Charge.

I. - I am to admonish you to honour God in his holy Church; that, you use no Heresy, Schism and Error in your Understandings, or discredit Men's Teachings.

II. - To be true to our Sovereign Lord the King, his Heirs and lawful Successors; committing no Treason, Misprision of Treason, or Felony; and if any Man shall commit Treason that you know of, you shall forthwith give Notice thereof to his Majesty, his Privy Counsellors, or some other Person that hath Commission to enquire thereof.

III. - You shall be true to your Fellows and Brethren of the Science of Masonry, and do unto them as you would be done unto.

IV. - You shall keep Secret the obscure and intricate Parts of the Science, not disclosing them to any but such as study and use the same.

V. - You shall do your Work truly and faithfully, endeavouring the Profit and Advantage of him that is Owner of the said Work.

VI. - You shall call Masons your Fellows and Brethren, without Addition of Knaves, or other bad Language.

VII. - You shall not take your Neighbour's Wife Willinously, nor his Daughter, nor his Maid or his Servant, to use ungodly.

VIII. - You shall not carnally lye with any Woman that is belonging to the House where you are at Table.

IX. - You shall truly pay for your Meat and Drink, where you are at Table.

X. - You shall not undertake any Man's Work, knowing yourself unable or unexpert to perform and effect the same, that no Discredit or Aspersion may be imputed to the Science, or the Lord or Owner of the said Work be any wise prejudic'd.

XI. - You shall not take any Work to do at excessive or unreasonable Rates, to deceive the Owner thereof, but so as he may be truly and faithfully serv'd with his own Goods.

XII. - You shall so take your Work, that thereby you may live honestly, and pay your Fellows the Wages as the Science doth require.

XIII. - You shall not supplant any of your Fellows of their Work, (that is to say) if he or any of them hath or have taken any Work upon him or them, or he or they stand Master or Masters of any Lord or Owner's Work, that you shall not put him or them out from the said Work, altho' you perceive him or them unable to finish the same.

XIV. - You shall not take any Apprentice to serve you in the said Science of *Masonry*, under the Term of Seven Years; nor any but such as are descended of good and honest Parentage, that no Scandal may be imputed to the said Science of *Masonry*.

XV. - You shall not take upon you to make any one *Mason* without the Privity or Consent of six, or five at least of your Fellows, and not but such as is Freeborn, and whose Parents live in good Fame and Name, and that hath his right and perfect Limbs, and able of Body to attend the said Science.

XVI. - You shall not pay any of your Fellows more Money than he or they have deserv'd, that you be not deceiv'd by slight or false Working, and the Owner thereof much wrong'd.

XVII. - You shall not slander any of your Fellows behind their Backs, to impair their Temporal Estate or good Name.

XVIII. - You shall not, without very urgent Cause, answer your Fellow doggedly or ungodly, but as becomes a loving Brother in the said Science.

XIX. - You shall duly reverence your Fellows, that the Bond of Charity and mutual Love may continue stedfast and stable amongst you.

XX. - You shall not (except in *Christmas* time) use any lawless Games, as Dice, Cards, or such like.

XXI. - You shall not frequent any Houses of Bawdery, or be a Pander to any of your Fellows or others, which will be a great Scandal to the Science.

XXII. - You shall not go out to drink by Night, or if Occasion happen that you must go, you shall not stay past Eight of the Clock, having some of your Fellows, or one at the least, to bear you Witness of the honest Place you were in, and your good Behaviour, to avoid Scandal.

XXIII. - You shall come to the Yearly Assembly, if you know where it is kept, being within Ten Miles of the Place of your Abode, submitting your self to the Censure of your Fellows, wherein you have ………. to make satisfaction, or else to defend by Order of the King's Laws.

XXIV. - You shall not make any Mould, Square, or Rule to mould Stones withal, but such as are allowed by the Fraternity.

XXV. - You shall set Strangers at Work, having Employment for them, at least a Fortnight, and pay them their Wages truly, and if you want Work for them, then you shall relieve them with Money to defray their reasonable Charges to the next Lodge.

XXVI. - You shall truly attend your Work, and truly end the same, whether it be Task or Journey-Work, if you may have the Payment and Wages according to your Agreement made with the Master or Owner thereof.

All these Articles and Charge, which I have now read unto you, you shall well and truly observe, perform and keep to the best of your Power, and Knowledge, So help you God, and the true and holy Contents of this Book.

And moreover I A. B. do here in the Presence of God Almighty and of my Fellows and Brethren here present, promise and declare, That I will not at any Time hereafter by any Act or Circumstance whatsoever, directly or indirectly, publish, discover, reveal or make known any of these Secrets, Privities or Councils of the Fraternity or Fellowship of Free-Masons, which at this time, or at any time hereafter shall be made known unto me.

So help me God, and the true and holy Contents of this Book.

This Charge belongeth to Apprentices.

Imprimis. - YOU shall truly honour God, and his holy Church, the King, your Master, and Dame; you shall not absent yourself, but with the Licence of one or both of them, from their Service, by Day or Night.

II. - You shall not Purloyn or Steal, or be Privy or accessary to the Purloyning or Stealing to the Value of Six-pence from them or either of them.

III. - You shall not commit Adultery or Fornication in the House of your Master, with his Wife, Daughter or Maid.

IV. - You shall not disclose your Master's or Dame's Secrets or Councils, which they have reported unto you, or what is to be concealed, spoken or done within the Privities of their House, by them, or either of them, or by any *Free-Mason*.

V. - You shall not maintain any disobedient Argument with your Master, Dame, or any *Free-Mason*.

VI. - You shall reverently behave your self towards all *Free-Masons*, using neither Cards, Dice, or any other unlawful Games, *Christmas* Time excepted.

VII. - You shall not haunt, or frequent any Taverns or Ale-houses, or so much as go into any of them, except it be upon your Master or your Dame, their or any of their Affairs, or with their or the one of their Consents.

VIII. - You shall not commit Adultery or Fornication in any Man's House, where you shall be at Table or at Work.

IX. - You shall not marry, or contract yourself to any Woman during your Apprenticeship.

X. - You shall not steal any Man's Goods, but especially your Master's, or any of his Fellow *Masons*, nor suffer any to steal their Goods, but shall hinder the Felon, if you can; and if you cannot, then you shall acquaint the said Master and his Fellows presently.

Additional Orders and Constitutions
Made and agreed upon at a General Assembly held at ....,
on the Eighth Day of December, 1663.

I. - THAT no Person, of what Degree soever, be accepted a *Free-Mason*, unless he shall have a Lodge of five *Free-Masons* at the least, whereof one to be a Master or Warden of that Limit or Division where such Lodge shall be kept, and another to be a Workman of the Trade of *Free-Masonry*.

II. - That no Person hereafter shall be accepted a *Free-Mason*, but such as are of able Body, honest Parentage, good Reputation, and Observers of the Laws of the Land.

III. - That no Person hereafter, which shall be accepted a *Free-Mason*, shall be admitted into any Lodge, or Assembly, until he hath brought a Certificate of the Time and Place of his Acception, from the Lodge that accepted him, unto the Master of that Limit and Division, where such Lodge was kept, which said Master shall enroll the same on Parchment in a Roll to be kept for that Purpose, and give an Account of all such Acceptions, at every General Assembly.

IV. - That every Person, who is now a *Free-Mason*, shall bring to the Master a Note of the Time of his Acception, to the end the same may be enrolled in such Priority of Place, as the Person deserves, and to the end the whole Company and Fellows may the better know each other.

V. - That for the future the said Society, Company and Fraternity of *Free-Masons*, shall be regulated and governed by one Master, and as many Wardens as the said Company shall think fit to chuse at every Yearly General Assembly.

VI. - That no Person shall be accepted a *Free-Mason*, unless he be One and Twenty Years Old, or more.

VII. - That no person hereafter be accepted a *Free-Mason*, or know the Secrets of the said Society, until he shall have first taken the Oath of Secrecy here following, viz.

I *A. B.* do here in the Presence of God Almighty, and of my Fellows and Bretheren here present, promise and declare, That I will not at any Time hereafter by any Act or Circumstance whatsoever directly or indirectly, publish, discover, reveal or make known any of the Secrets, Privities or Councils of the Fraternity or Fellowship of Free Masons, which at this time, or at any time hereafter shall be made known unto me.

So help me God, and the true and holy Contents of this Book.

FINIS.

Ancient Charges of a FREE MASON
as contained in Anderson's Constitutions of the Freemasons, published 1723

The Ancient Records of Lodges beyond the Sea

To Be Read At The Making of New Brethren, or When The Master Shall Order It. THE GENERAL HEADS, viz.:

I. Concerning GOD and RELIGION.

A Mason is oblig'd by his Tenure, to obey the moral law; and if he rightly understands the Art, he will never be a stupid Atheist nor an irreligious Libertine. But though in ancient Times Masons were charg'd in every Country to be of the Religion of that Country or Nation, whatever it was, yet 'tis now thought more expedient only to oblige them to that Religion in which all Men agree, leaving their particular Opinions to themselves; that is, to be good Men and true, or Men of Honour and Honesty, by whatever Denominations or Persuasions they may be distinguish'd; whereby Masonry becomes the Center of Union, and the Means of conciliating true Friendship among Persons that must have remain'd at a perpetual Distance.

II Of the CIVIL MAGISTRATES SUPREME and SUBORDINATE.

A Mason is a peaceable Subject to the Civil Powers, wherever he resides or works, and is never to be concern'd in Plots an Conspiracies against the Peace and Welfare of the Nation, nor to behave himself undutifully to inferior Magistrates; for as Masonry hath been always injured by War, Bloodshed, and Confusion, so ancient Kings and Princes have been much dispos'd to encourage the Craftsmen, because of their Peaceableness and Loyalty, whereby they practically answer'd the Cavils of their Adversaries, and promoted the Honour of the Fraternity, who ever flourish'd in Time of Peace. So that if a Brother should be a Rebel against the State he is not to be countenanced in his Rebellion, however he may be pitied as any unhappy Man; and, if convicted of no other Crime though the Loyal Brotherhood must and ought to disown hi Rebellion, and give no

Ancient Charges of a FREE MASON

Umbrage or Ground of political Jealousy to the Government for the time being, they cannot expel him from the Lodge, and his Relation to it remains indefeasible.

III Of LODGES.

A Lodge is a place where Masons assemble and work; Hence that Assembly, or duly organized Society of Masons, is call'd a Lodge, and every Brother ought to belong to one, and to be subject to its By-Laws and the General Regulations.

It is either particular or general, and will be best understood by attending it, and by the Regulations of the General or Grand Lodge hereunto annex'd. In ancient Times, no Master or Fellow could be absent from it especially when warned to appear at it, without incurring a sever Censure, until it appear'd to the Master and Wardens that pure Necessity hinder'd him.

The persons admitted Members of a Lodge must be good an true Men, free-born, and of mature and discreet Age, no Bondmen no Women, no immoral or scandalous men, but of good Report.

IV Of MASTERS, WARDENS, FELLOWS and APPRENTICES.

All preferment among Masons is grounded upon real Worth and personal Merit only; that so the Lords may be well served, the Brethren not put to Shame, nor the Royal Craft despis'd: Therefore no Master or Warden is chosen by Seniority, but for his Merit. It is impossible to describe these things in Writing, and every Brother must attend in his Place, and learn them in a Way peculiar to this Fraternity: Only Candidates may know that no Master should take an Apprentice unless he has Sufficient Employment for him, and unless he be a perfect Youth having no Maim or Defects in his Body that may render him uncapable of learning the Art of serving his Master's Lord, and of being made a Brother, and then a Fellow-Craft in due Time, even after he has served such a Term of Years as the Custom of the Country directs; and that he should be descended of honest Parents; that so, when otherwise qualifi'd he may arrive to the

Honour of being the Warden, and then the Master of the Lodge, the Grand Warden, and at length the Grand Master of all the Lodges, according to his Merit.

No Brother can be a Warden until he has pass'd the part of a Fellow-Craft; nor a Master until he has acted as a Warden, nor Grand Warden until he has been Master of a Lodge, nor Grand Master unless he has been a Fellow Craft before his Election, who is also to be nobly born, or a Gentleman of the best Fashion, or some eminent Scholar, or some curious Architect, or other Artist, descended of honest Parents, and who is of similar great Merit in the Opinion of the Lodges.

These Rulers and Governors, supreme and subordinate, of the ancient Lodge, are to be obey'd in their respective Stations by all the Brethren, according to the old Charges and Regulations, with all Humility, Reverence, Love and Alacrity.

V. Of the MANAGEMENT of the CRAFT in WORKING.

All Masons shall work honestly on Working Days, that they may live creditably on Holy Days; and the time appointed by the Law of the Land or confirm'd by Custom shall be observ'd. The most expert of the Fellow-Craftsmen shall be chosen or appointed the Master or Overseer of the Lord's Work; who is to be call'd Master by those that work under him. The Craftsmen are to avoid all ill Language, and to call each other by no disobliging Name, but Brother or Fellow; and to behave themselves courteously within and without the Lodge.

The Master, knowing himself to be able of Cunning, shall undertake the Lord's Work as reasonably as possible, and truly dispend his Goods as if they were his own; nor to give more Wages to any Brother or Apprentice than he really may deserve.

Both the Master and the Masons receiving their Wages justly, shall be faithful to the Lord and honestly finish their Work, whether Task or journey; nor put the work to Task that hath been accustomed to Journey.

None shall discover Envy at the Prosperity of a Brother, nor supplant him, or put him out of his Work, if he be capable to finish the same; for no man can finish another's Work so much to the Lord's Profit, unless he be thoroughly acquainted with the Designs and Draughts of him that began it.

When a Fellow-Craftsman is chosen Warden of the Work under the Master, he shall be true both to Master and Fellows, shall carefully oversee the Work in the Master's Absence to the Lord's profit; and his Brethren shall obey him.

All Masons employed shall meekly receive their Wages without Murmuring or Mutiny, and not desert the Master till the Work is finish'd.

A younger Brother shall be instructed in working, to prevent spoiling the Materials for want of Judgment, and for increasing and continuing of brotherly love.

All the Tools used in working shall be approved by the Grand Lodge.

No Laborer shall be employ'd in the proper Work of Masonry; nor shall Free Masons work with those that are not free, without an urgent Necessity; nor shall they teach Laborers and unaccepted Masons as they should teach a Brother or Fellow.

VI. Of BEHAVIOR.

I. In the LODGE while CONSTITUTED.

You are not to hold private Committees, or separate Conversation without Leave from the Master, nor to talk of anything impertinent or unseemly, nor interrupt the Master or Wardens, or any Brother speaking to the Master: Nor behave yourself ludicrously or jestingly while the Lodge is engaged in what is serious and solemn; nor use any unbecoming Language upon any Pretense whatsoever; but to pay due Reverence to your Master, Wardens, and Fellows, and put them to Worship.

If any Complaint be brought, the Brother found guilty shall stand to the Award and Determination of the Lodge, who are the proper and competent Judges of all such Controversies (unless you carry it by Appeal to the Grand Lodge), and to whom they ought to be referr'd, unless a Lord's Work be hinder'd the meanwhile, in which Case a particular Reference may be made; but you must never go to Law about what concerneth Masonry, without an absolute necessity apparent to the Lodge.

2. BEHAVIOR after the LODGE is over and the BRETHREN not GONE.

You may enjoy yourself with innocent Mirth, treating one another according to Ability, but avoiding all Excess, or forcing any Brother to eat or drink beyond his Inclination, or hindering him from going when his Occasions call him, or doing or saying anything offensive, or that may forbid an easy and free Conversation, for that would blast our Harmony, and defeat our laudable Purposes. Therefore no private Piques or Quarrels must be brought within the Door of the Lodge, far less any Quarrels about Religion, or Nations, or State Policy, we being only, as Masons, of the Universal Religion above mention'd, we are also of all Nations, Tongues, Kindreds, and Languages, and are resolv'd against all Politics, as what never yet conduct'd to the Welfare of the Lodge, nor ever will.

3. BEHAVIOR when BRETHREN meet WITHOUT STRANGERS, but not in a LODGE Formed.

You are to salute one another in a courteous Manner, as you will be instructed, calling each other Brother, freely giving mutual instruction as shall be thought expedient, without being ever seen or overheard, and without encroaching upon each other, or derogating from that Respect which is due to any Brother, were he not Mason: For though all Masons are as Brethren upon the same Level, yet Masonry takes no Honour from a man that he had before; nay, rather it adds to his Honour, especially if he has deserve well of the Brotherhood, who must give Honor to whom it is due, and avoid ill Manners.

4. BEHAVIOR in presence of Strangers NOT MASONS.

You shall be cautious in your Words and Carriage, that the most penetrating Stranger shall not be able to discover or find out what is not proper to be intimated, and sometimes you shall divert a Discourse, and manage it prudently for the Honour of the worshipful Fraternity.

5. BEHAVIOR at HOME, and in Your NEIGHBORHOOD.

You are to act as becomes a moral and wise Man; particularly not to let your Family, Friends and Neighbors know the Concern of the Lodge, &c., but wisely to consult your own Honour, and that of the ancient Brotherhood, for reasons not to be mention'd here You must also consult your Health, by not continuing together too late, or too long from Home, after Lodge Hours are past; and by avoiding of Gluttony or Drunkenness, that your Families be not neglected or injured, nor you disabled from working.

6. BEHAVIOR toward a Strange BROTHER.

You are cautiously to examine him, in such a Method as Prudence shall direct you, that you may not be impos'd upon by an ignorant, false Pretender, whom you are to reject with contempt and Derision, and beware of giving him any Hints of Knowledge.

But if you discover him to be a true and genuine Brother, you are to respect him accordingly; and if he is in Want, you must relieve him if you can, or else direct him how he may be relieved; you must employ him some days, or else recommend him to be employ'd. But you are not charged to do beyond your ability, only to prefer a poor Brother, that is a good Man and true before any other poor People in the same Circumstance.

Finally, All these Charges you are to observe, and also those that shall be recommended to you in another Way; cultivating Brotherly Love, the Foundation and Cap-stone, the Cement and Glory of this Ancient Fraternity, avoiding all wrangling and quarreling, all

Slander and Backbiting, nor permitting others to slander any honest Brother, but defending his Character, and doing him all good Offices, as far as is consistent with your Honour and Safety, and no farther. And if any of them do you Injury you must apply to your own or his Lodge, and from thence you may appeal to the Grand Lodge, at the Quarterly Communication and from thence to the annual Grand Lodge, as has been the ancient laudable Conduct but when the Case cannot be otherwise decided, and patiently listening to the honest and friendly Advice of Master and Fellows when they would prevent your going to Law with Strangers, or would excite you to put a speedy Period to all Lawsuits, so that you may mind the Affair of Masonry with the more Alacrity and Success; but with respect to Brothers or Fellows at Law, the Master and Brethren should kindly offer their Mediation, which ought to be thankfully submitted to by the contending Brethren; and if that submission is impracticable, they must, however, carry on their Process, or Lawsuit, without Wrath and Rancor (not In the common way) saying or doing nothing which may hinder Brotherly Love, and good Offices to be renew'd and continu'd; that all may see the benign Influence of Masonry, as all true Masons have done from the beginning of the World, and will do to the End of Time.

Amen, So Mote It Be

General Regulations of a Freemason
as contained in Anderson's Constitutions of the Freemasons, published 1723

Compiled first by Mr. George Payne, Anno 1720, when he was Grand Master, and approv'd by the Grand Lodge on St. John Baptist's Day, Anno 1721; at Stationer's Hall, London; when the most noble Prince John, Duke of Montagu, was unanimously chosen our Grand Master for the Year ensuing; who chose, John Beal, M.D., his Deputy Grand Master:

And were chosen by the Lodge [as] Grand Wardens:
Mr. Josiah Villeneau,
Mr. Thomas Morris, Jun.

And now, by the Command of our said Right Worshipful Grand Master Montagu, the Author of this Book has compar'd them with, and reduc'd them to the ancient Records and immemorial Usage of the Fraternity, and digested them into this new Method with several proper Explications for the use of the Lodges in and about Westminster.

I. The Grand Master or his Deputy hath Authority and Right not only to be present in any true Lodge, but also to preside wherever he is, with the Master of the Lodge on his Left Hand, an to order his Grand Wardens to attend him, who are not to act in particular Lodges as Wardens, but in his Presence, and at his Command: because there the Grand Master may command the Wardens of that Lodge, or any other Brethren he pleaseth, to attend and act as his Wardens pro tempore.

II. The Master of a particular Lodge, has the right and authority of congregating the Members of his Lodge into a Chapter at Pleasure, upon any Emergency or Occurrence as well as to appoint the Time and Place of their usual forming: And in Case of Sickness Death, or necessary Absence of the Master, the Senior Warden shall act as Master pro tempore, if no Brother is present who has been Master of that Lodge before; for in that Case the absent Master's Authority reverts to the last Master then present; though he cannot act until the Senior Warden has once congregated the Lodge or in his Absence the Junior Warden.

III. The Master of each particular Lodge, or one of the Wardens, or some other Brother by his Order, shall keep a Book containing their By-Laws, the Names of their Members, with a list of all the Lodges in Town, and the usual Times and places of their forming, and all their Transactions that are proper to be written

IV. No Lodge shall make more than Five new Brethren at one Time, nor any Man under the Age of Twenty-five, who must be also his own Master; unless by a Dispensation from the Grand Master or his Deputy.

V. No man can be made or admitted a Member of a particular Lodge, without previous Notice one Month before given to the said Lodge, in order to make due Inquiry into the Reputation and Capacity of the Candidate; unless by the Dispensation aforesaid.

VI. But no man can enter'd a Brother in any particular Lodge, or admitted to be a Member thereof, without the unanimous Consent of all the Members of that Lodge then present when the Candidate is propos'd, and their Consent is formally ask'd by the Master; and they are to signify their Consent or Dissent in their own Prudent Way, either virtually or in form, but with Unanimity: Nor is this inherent Privilege subject to a Dispensation; because the Members of a particular Lodge are the best Judges of it; and if a fractious Member should be impos'd on them, it might spoil their Harmony, or hinder their Freedom; or even break and disperse the Lodge, which ought to be avoided by all good and true Brethren.

VII. Every new Brother at his making is recently to cloath the Lodge, that is, all the Brethren present, and to deposit something for the Relief of indigent and decay'd Brethren, as the Candidate shall think fit to bestow, over and above the small allowance stated by the By-Laws of that particular Lodge, which Charity shall be lodg'd with the Master or Wardens, or the Cashier, if the Members see fit to chuse one. And the Candidate shall also solemnly promise to submit to the Constitution, the Charges and Regulations, and to such other good Usages as shall be intimated to them in Time and Place convenient.

VIII. No set or Number of Brethren shall withdraw or separate themselves from the Lodge in which they were made Brethren, or were afterwards admitted Members, unless the Lodge becomes too numerous; nor even then, without a Dispensation from the Grand Master or his Deputy; and when they are thus separated, they must either immediately join themselves to such other Lodge as they shall like best, with the unanimous Consent of that other Lodge to which they go (as above regulated), or else they must obtain the Grand Master's Warrant to join in forming a new Lodge.

If any set or Number of Masons shall take upon themselves to form a Lodge without the Grand Master's Warrant, the regular Lodges are not to countenance them, or own them as fair brethren and duly form'd, nor approve of their Acts and Deeds; but must treat them as Rebels, until they humble themselves, as the Grand Master, shall, in his Prudence, direct, and until he approve of them by his Warrant, which must be signified to the other Lodges, as the Custom is when a new Lodge is to be registered in the List of Lodges.

IX. But if any Brother so far misbehave himself as to render his Lodge uneasy, he shall be twice duly admonished by the Master or Wardens in a form'd Lodge; and if he will not refrain his Imprudence, and obediently submit to the Advice of the Brethren, and reform what gives them Offense, he shall be dealt with according to the By-Laws of that particular Lodge, or else in such a manner as the Quarterly Communication shall in their great prudence think fit; for which a new Regulation may be afterward made.

X. The Majority of every particular Lodge, when congregated, shall have the Privilege of giving Instructions to their Masters and Wardens before the assembling of the Grand Chapter or Lodge, at the three Quarterly Communications hereafter mention'd and of the annual Grand Lodge, too; because their Master and Wardens are their Representatives, and are supposed to speak their mind.

XI. All particular Lodges are to observe the same usages as much as possible; in order to which, and for cultivating a good Understanding among Free-Masons, some members out of every Lodge shall be deputed to visit the other Lodges as often as shall be thought convenient.

XII. The Grand Lodge consists of, and is form'd by, the Masters and Wardens of all the regular particular Lodges upon Record, with the Grand Master at their Head, and his Deputy on his Left hand, and the Grand Wardens in their proper places; and must have a Quarterly

Communication about Michaelmas, Christmas and Lady Day, in some convenient Place, as the Grand Master shall appoint, where no Brother shall be present, who is not at that time a Member thereof, without a Dispensation; and while he stays, he shall not be allow'd to vote, nor even given his Opinion without Leave of the Grand Lodge ask'd and given, or unless it be duly ask'd by the said Lodge.

All matters are to be determined in the Grand Lodge by a Majority of Votes, each member having one Vote, and the Grand Master having two Votes, unless the said Lodge leave any particular thing to the Determination of the Grand Master for the sake of Expedition.

XIII. At the said Quarterly Communication all Masters that concern the Fraternity in general, or particular Lodges, or single Brethren, are quietly, sedately and maturely to be discoursed and transacted; Apprentices must be admitted Masters and Fellow-Craft only here, unless by a Dispensation. Here also all differences, that cannot be made up and accommodated privately, nor by a particular Lodge, are to be seriously considered and decided: And if any Brother thinks himself aggrieved by the Decision of this Board, he may Appeal to the annual Grand Lodge next ensuing, and leave his Appeal in Writing with the Grand Master, or his Deputy, or the Grand Wardens.

Here also the Master or the Wardens of each particular Lodge shall bring and produce a List of such Members as have been made or even admitted in their particular Lodges since the last Communication of the Grand Lodge. And there shall be a book kept by the Grand Master, or his Deputy, or rather by some Brother whom the Grand Lodge shall appoint for Secretary, wherein shall be recorded all the Lodges, with their usual Times and Places of forming, and the Names of all the Members of each Lodge; and all the Affairs of the Grand Lodge that are proper to be written.

They shall also consider of the most prudent and effectual Methods of collecting and disposing of what Money shall be given to, or Lodged with them in Charity, towards the Relief only of any true Brother fallen into poverty or Decay, but of none else. But every particular Lodge shall dispose of their own Charity for poor Brethren, according to their own By-Laws, until it be agreed by all the Lodges (in a new Regulation) to carry in the Charity collection by them to the

General Regulations of a Freemason

Grand Lodge, at the Quarterly or Annual Communication, in order to make a common Stock of it, for the more handsome Relief of poor Brethren.

They shall appoint a Treasurer, a Brother of good worldly Substance, who shall be a Member of the Grand Lodge by virtue of his Office, and shall be always present, and have Power to move to the Grand Lodge anything, especially what concerns his Office. To him shall be committed all Money rais'd for Charity, or for any other Use of the Grand Lodge, which he shall write down in a book, with the respective Ends and Uses for which the several Sums are intended; and shall expend or disburse the same by such a certain Order sign'd, as the Grand Lodge shall afterwards agree to in a new Regulation: But he shall not vote in chusing a Grand Master or Wardens, though in every other Transaction. As in like manner the Secretary shall be a Member of the Grand Lodge by virtue of his Office, and vote in everything except in chusing a Grand Master or Wardens.

The Treasurer and Secretary shall have each a Clerk, who must be a Brother and Fellow-Craft, but never must be a member of the Grand Lodge, nor speak without being allow'd or desir'd.

The Grand Master or his Deputy, shall always command the Treasurer and Secretary, with their Clerks and Books in order to see how Matters go on, and to know what is expedient to be done upon any emergent Occasion.

Another Brother (who must be a Fellow-Craft) should be appointed to look after the Door of the Grand Lodge; but shall be no member of it.

But these Officers may be farther explain'd by a new Regulation, when the Necessity and Expediency of them may more appear than at present to the Fraternity.

XIV. If at any Grand Lodge, stated or occasional, quarterly or annual, the Grand Master and his Deputy should be both absent, then the present Master of a Lodge, that has been the longest a Free Mason, shall take the Chair, and preside as Grand Master pro tempore; and shall be vested with all his Power and Honour for the time; provided there is no Brother present that has been Grand Master formerly, or Deputy Grand Master; for the last Grand Master present, or else the last Deputy present, should always of right take place in the Absence of the present Grand Master and his Deputy.

XV. In the Grand Lodge none can act as Wardens but the Grand Wardens themselves, if present; and if absent, the Grand Master, or the Person who presides in his place, shall order private Wardens to act as Grand Wardens pro tempore, whose Places are to be suppli'd by two Fellow-Craft of the same Lodge, call'd forth to act, or sent thither by the particular Master thereof; or if by him omitted, then they shall be call'd by the Grand Master, that so the Grand Lodge may be always complete.

XVI. The Grand Wardens, or any others, are first to advise with the Deputy about the Affairs of the Lodge or of the Brethren, and not to apply to the Grand Master without the knowledge of the Deputy, unless he refuse his Concurrence in any certain necessary affair; in which Case, or in case of any Difference between the Deputy and the Grand Wardens or other Brethren both parties are to go by Concert to the Grand Master, who can easily decide the Controversy and make up the Difference by virtue of his great Authority.

The Grand Master should receive no Intimation of Business concerning Masonry, but from his Deputy first, except in such certain Cases as his Worship can well judge of; for if the Application the Grand Master be irregular, he can easily order the Grand Wardens or any other Brethren thus applying, to wait upon his Deputy, who is to prepare the Business speedily, and to lay it orderly before his Worship.

XVII. No Grand Master, Deputy Grand Master, Grand Wardens, Treasurer, Secretary, or whoever acts for them, or in their stead pro tempore, can at the same time be the Master or Warden of a particular Lodge; but as soon as any of them has honorably discharg'd his Grand Office, he returns to that post or station in his particular Lodge, from which he was call'd to officiate above.

XVIII. If the Deputy Grand Master be sick, or necessarily absent, the Grand Master may chuse any Fellow-Craft he pleases to be his Deputy pro tempore: But he that is chosen Deputy at the Grand Lodge, and the Grand Wardens, too, cannot be discharged without the Cause fairly appear to the Majority of the Grand Lodge; and the Grand Master, if he is uneasy, may call a Grand Lodge on purpose to lay the Case before them, and to have their Advise and Concurrence.

In which case the Majority of the Grand Lodge, if they cannot reconcile the Master and his Deputy or his Wardens, are to concur in allowing the Master to discharge his said Deputy or his said Wardens, and to chuse another Deputy immediately; and the said Grand Lodge shall chuse other Wardens in that Case, that Harmony and Peace may be preserved.

XIX. If the Grand Master should abuse his Power, and render himself unworthy of the Obedience and Subjection of the Lodges, he shall be treated in a way and manner to be agreed upon in a new Regulation; because hitherto the ancient Fraternity have had no occasion for it, their former Grand Masters having all behaved themselves worthy of that honorable Office.

XX. The Grand Master, with his Deputy and Wardens, shall (at least once) go around and visit all the Lodges about Town during his Mastership.

XXI. If the Grand Master die during his Mastership, or by Sickness, or by Being beyond Sea, or any other way should be render'd uncapable of discharging his Office, the Deputy, in his Absence, the Senior Grand Warden, or in his Absence, the Junior, or in his Absence any three present Masters of Lodges, shall join to congregate the Grand Lodge immediately, to advise together upon that Emergency, and to send two of their Number to invite the last Grand Master to resume his office, which now in course reverts to him; or if he refuse, then the next last, and so backward: But if no former Grand Master can be found, then the Deputy shall act as Principal until another is chosen; or if there be no Deputy, then the oldest Master.

XXII. The Brethren of all the Lodges in and about London and Westminster, shall meet at an Annual Communication and Feast, in some convenient place, on St. John Baptist's Day, or else on St. John Evangelist's Day, as the Grand Lodge shall think fit by a new Regulation, having of late Years met on St. John Baptist's Day. Provided, The Majority of the Masters and Wardens with the Grand Master, his Deputy and Wardens, agree at their Quarterly Communication, three months before, that there shall be a Feast, and a General Communication of all Brethren: For if either the Grand Master, or the Majority of the particular Masters, are against it, it must be dropt for that Time.

But whether there shall be a Feast for all the Brethren, or not, yet the Grand Lodge must meet in some convenient Place annually on St. John's Day; or if it be Sunday, then on the next Day, in order to chuse every Year a new Grand Master, Deputy and Warden.

XXIII. If it be thought expedient, and the Grand Master, with the Majority of the Masters and Wardens, agree to hold a Grand Feast according to the ancient laudable Custom of Masons, then the Grand Wardens shall have the care of preparing the Tickets, seal'd with the Grand Master's Seal, of disposing of the Tickets, of receiving the money for the Tickets, of buying the Materials of the Feast, of finding out a proper and convenient Place to feast in; and of every other thing that concerns the Entertainment.

But that the Work may not be too burthensome to the two Grand Wardens, and that all Matters may be expeditiously and safely managed, the Grand Master or his Deputy shall have power to nominate and appoint a certain Number of Stewards, as his Worship shall think fit, to act in concert with the two Grand Wardens; all things relating to the Feast being decided among them by a Majority of Voices; except the Grand Master or his Deputy interpose by a particular Direction of Appointment.

XXIV. The Wardens and Stewards shall, in due time, wait upon the Grand Master or his Deputy for Directions and Orders about the Premises; but if his Worship and his Deputy are sick, or necessarily absent, they shall call together the Masters and Wardens of Lodges to meet on purpose for their Advice and Orders; or else they may take the Matter wholly upon themselves and do the best they can.

The Grand Wardens and the Stewards are to account for all the Money they receive, or expend, to the Grand Lodge, after dinner, or when the Grand Lodge shall think fit to receive their Accounts.

If the Grand Master pleases, he may in due time summons all the Masters and Wardens of Lodges to consult with them about ordering the Grand Feast, and about any Emergency or accidental thing relating thereunto, that may require Advice; or else to take it upon himself altogether.

XXV. The Masters of Lodges shall each appoint one experienced and discreet Fellow-Craft of his Lodge, to compose a Committee, consisting of one from every Lodge, who shall meet to receive, in a convenient Apartment, every Person that brings a Ticket, and shall have Power to discourse him, if they think fit, in order to admit him or debar him, as they shall see cause; Provided they send no Man away before they have acquainted all the Brethren within Doors with the Reasons thereof, to avoid Mistakes, that so no true Brother may be debarr'd, nor a false Brother, or more Pretender, admitted. This Committee must meet very early on St. John's Day at the Place, even before any Person come with Tickets.

XXVI. The Grand Master shall appoint two or more trusty Brethren to be Porters or Door-Keepers, who are also to be early at the Place, for some good Reasons; and who are to be at the Command of the Committee.

XXVII. The Grand Wardens, or the Stewards, shall appoint before hand such a Number of Brethren to serve at Table as they think fit and proper for that Work; and they may advise with the Masters and Wardens of Lodges about the most proper Persons, if they please, or may take in such by their Recommendation; for none are to serve that Day but free and accepted Masons, that the Communication may be free and harmonious.

XXVIII. All the Members of the Grand Lodge must be at the Place long before Dinner, with the Grand Master or his Deputy at their Head, who shall retire and form themselves. And this is done in order:

1. To receive any Appeals duly lodg'd, as above regulated, that the appellant may be heard, and the Affair may be amicably decided before Dinner, if possible; but if it cannot, it must be delay'd till after the new Grand Master is elected; and if it cannot be decided after Dinner, it may be delay'd and referr'd to a particular Committee, that shall quietly adjust it, and make Report to the next Quarterly Communication, that Brotherly Love may be preserved.

2. To prevent any Difference or Disgust which may be feared to arise that Day; that no Interruption maybe given to the Harmony and Pleasure of the Grand Feast.

3. To consult about whatever concerns the Decency and Decorum of the Grand Assembly, and to prevent all Indecency and ill Manners, the Assembly being promiscuous.

4. To receive and consider of any good Motion, or any momentous and important Affair, that shall be brought from the

particular Lodges, by their Representatives, the several Masters and Wardens.

XXIX. After these things are discuss'd, the Grand Master and his Deputy, the Grand Wardens, or the Stewards, the Secretary, the Treasurer, the Clerks, and every other Person shall withdraw, and leave the Masters and Wardens of the Particular Lodges alone, in, order to consult amicably about electing a new Grand Master, or continuing the present, if they have not done it the Day before; and if they are unanimous for continuing the present Grand Master, his Worship shall be call'd in, and humbly desir'd to do the Fraternity the Honour of ruling them for the Year ensuing. And after Dinner it will be known whether he accept of it or not: For it should not be discovered but by the Election itself.

XXX. Then the Master and Wardens and all the Brethren, may converse promiscuously, or as they please to sort together, until the Dinner is coming in, when every Brother takes his Seat at the Table.

XXXI. Some time after Dinner the Grand Lodge is form'd, not in Retirement, but in the Presence of all the Brethren, who yet are not Members of it, and must not therefore speak until they are desir'd and allowed.

XXXII. If the Grand Master of last Year has consented with the Masters and Wardens in private, before Dinner, to continue for the Year ensuing; then one of the Grand Lodge, deputed for that Purpose, shall represent to all the Brethren his Worship's good Government, &c. And turning to him, shall, in the name of the Grand Lodge, humbly request him to do the Fraternity the great Honour (if nobly born, if not) the great Kindness, of continuing to be their Grand Master for the Year ensuing. And his Worship declaring his consent by a Bow or a Speech, as he pleases, the said deputed Member of the Grand Lodge shall proclaim him Grand Master, and all the Members of the Lodge shall salute him in due Form. And all the Brethren shall for a few minutes have leave to declare their Satisfaction, Pleasure and Congratulation.

XXXIII. But if either the Masters and Wardens have not in private, this Day before Dinner, nor the Day before, desir'd the last Grand Master to continue in the Mastership another Year, or if he, when desir'd, has not consented: Then,

The last Grand Master shall nominate his Successor for the year ensuing, who, if unanimously approv'd by the Grand Lodge and if there present, shall be proclaim'd, saluted, and congratulated, the new Grand Master as above hinted, and immediately installed by the last Grand Master, according to Usage.

XXXIV. But if that Nomination is not unanimously approv'd, the new Grand Master shall be chosen immediately by Ballot, every Master and Warden writing his Man's name, and the last Grand Master writing his Man's Name too; and the Man whose name the last Grand Master shall first take out, casually or by chance, shall be Grand Master for the Year ensuing; and if present, he shall be proclaim'd, saluted, and congratulated, as above hinted, and forthwith installed by the last Grand Master, according to Usage.

XXXV. The last Grand Master thus continued, or the New Grand Master thus installed, shall next nominate and appoint his Deputy Grand Master, either the last or a new one, who shall be also declar'd, saluted, and congratulated as above hinted.

The Grand Master shall also nominate the new Grand Wardens, and if unanimously approv'd by the Grand Lodge, shall be declar'd, saluted, and congratulated, as above hinted; but if not, they shall be chosen by Ballot, in the same way as the Grand Master: And the Wardens of private Lodges are also to be chosen by Ballot in each Lodge, if the Members thereof do not agree to their Master's Nomination.

XXXVI. But If the Brother, whom the present Grand Master shall nominate for his Successor, or whom the Majority of the Grand Lodge shall happen to chuse by Ballot is, by sickness, or other necessary Occasion, absent from the Grand Feast, he cannot be proclaimed the New Grand Master, unless the old Grand Master, or some of the Masters and Wardens of the Grand Lodge can vouch, upon the Honour of a Brother, that the said Person, so nominated or chosen, will readily accept of the said Office; in which case the old Grand Master shall act as Proxy, and shall nominate the Deputy and Wardens in his Name, and in his name also receive the usual Honours. Homage, and Congratulation.

XXXVII. Then the Grand Master shall allow any Brother, Fellow-Craft, or Apprentice to speak, Directing his Discourse to his Worship; or to make any motion for the good of the Fraternity, which shall be either immediately consider'd and finish'd, or also referr'd to the Consideration of the Grand Lodge at their next communication, stated or occasional. When that is over.

XXXVIII. The Grand Master or his Deputy, or some Brother appointed by him, shall harangue all the Brethren, and give them good Advice: And lastly, after some other Transactions, that cannot be written in any language, the Brethren may go away or stay longer, as they please.

XXXIX. Every Annual Grand Lodge has an inherent Power and Authority to make new Regulations, or to alter these, for the real Benefits of this ancient Fraternity: Provided always that the old Land Marks be carefully preserv'd, and that such Alterations and new Regulations be proposed and agreed to at the third Quarterly Communication preceding the Annual Grand Feast, and that they be offered also to the Perusal of all the Brethren before Dinner, in writing, even of the youngest Apprentice, the Approbation and Consent of the Majority of all the Brethren present being absolutely necessary to make the same binding and obligatory; which must, after Dinner and after the new Grand Master is install'd, be solemnly desir'd; as it was desir'd and obtained for these Regulations, when propos'd by the Grand Lodge, to about 150 Brethren on St. John Baptist's Day, 1721.

The Graham Manuscript
circa 1726

original text

... we have it by tradition and still some referance to scripture cause shem ham and Japeth ffor to go to their father noahs grave for to try if they could find anything about him ffor to Lead them to the vertuable secret which this famieous preacher had for I hop all will allow that all things needfull for the new world was in the ark with noah Now these 3 men had allready agreed that if they did not ffind the verything it self that the first thing that they found was to be to them as a secret they not Doubting but did most ffirmly beLeive that God was able and would allso prove willing through their faith prayer and obediance for to cause what they did find for to prove as vertuable to them as if they had received the secret at first from God himself at its head spring so came to the Grave ffinding nothing save the dead body all most consumed away takeing a greip at a ffinger it came away so from Joynt to Joynt so to the wrest so to the Elbow so they RReared up the dead body and suported it setting ffoot to ffoot knee to knee Breast to breast cheek to cheek and hand to back and cryed out help o ffather as if they had said o father of heaven help us now for our Earthly ffather cannot so Laid down the dead body again and not knowing what to do — so one said here is yet marow in this bone and the second said but a dry bone and the third said it stinketh so they agreed ffor to give it a name as is known to free masonry to this day so went to their undertakings and afterwards works stood:yet it is to be beleived and allso understood that the vertue did not proceed from what they ffound or how it was called but ffrom ffaith and prayer so thus it Contenued the will pass for the deed.

Ancient Charges of a FREE MASON
as contained in Anderson's Constitutions of the Freemasons, published 1738

I. Concerning GOD and RELIGION.

A Mason is oblig'd by his Tenure, to obey the moral law; and if he rightly understands the Art, he will never be a stupid Atheist nor an irreligious Libertine. But though in ancient Times Masons were charg'd in every Country to be of the Religion of that Country or Nation, whatever it was, yet 'tis now thought more expedient only to oblige them to that Religion in which all Men agree, leaving their particular Opinions to themselves; that is, to be good Men and true, or Men of Honour and Honesty, by whatever Denominations or Persuasions they may be distinguish'd; whereby Masonry becomes the Center of Union, and the Means of conciliating true Friendship among Persons that must have remain'd at a perpetual Distance.

II Of the CIVIL MAGISTRATES SUPREME and SUBORDINATE.

A Mason is a peaceable Subject to the Civil Powers, wherever he resides or works, and is never to be concern'd in Plots an Conspiracies against the Peace and Welfare of the Nation, nor to behave himself undutifully to inferior Magistrates; for as Masonry hath been always injured by War, Bloodshed, and Confusion, so ancient Kings and Princes have been much dispos'd to encourage the Craftsmen, because of their Peaceableness and Loyalty, whereby they practically answer'd the Cavils of their Adversaries, and promoted the Honour of the Fraternity, who ever flourish'd in Time of Peace. So that if a Brother should be a Rebel against the State he is not to be countenanced in his Rebellion, however he may be pitied as any unhappy Man; and, if convicted of no other Crime though the Loyal Brotherhood must and ought to disown hi Rebellion, and give no Umbrage or Ground of political Jealousy to the Government for the time being, they cannot expel him from the Lodge, and his Relation to it remains indefeasible.

III Of LODGES.

A Lodge is a place where Masons assemble and work; Hence that Assembly, or duly organized Society of Masons, is call'd a Lodge, and every Brother ought to belong to one, and to be subject to its By-Laws and the General Regulations.

It is either particular or general, and will be best understood by attending it, and by the Regulations of the General or Grand Lodge hereunto annex'd. In ancient Times, no Master or Fellow could be absent from it especially when warned to appear at it, without incurring a sever Censure, until it appear'd to the Master and Wardens that pure Necessity hinder'd him.

The persons admitted Members of a Lodge must be good an true Men, free-born, and of mature and discreet Age, no Bondmen no Women, no immoral or scandalous men, but of good Report.

IV Of MASTERS, WARDENS, FELLOWS and APPRENTICES.

All preferment among Masons is grounded upon real Worth and personal Merit only; that so the Lords may be well served, the Brethren not put to Shame, nor the Royal Craft despis'd: Therefore no Master or Warden is chosen by Seniority, but for his Merit. It is impossible to describe these things in Writing, and every Brother must attend in his Place, and learn them in a Way peculiar to this Fraternity: Only Candidates may know that no Master should take an Apprentice unless he has Sufficient Employment for him, and unless he be a perfect Youth having no Maim or Defects in his Body that may render him uncapable of learning the Art of serving his Master's Lord, and of being made a Brother, and then a Fellow-Craft in due Time, even after he has served such a Term of Years as the Custom of the Country directs; and that he should be descended of honest Parents; that so, when otherwise qualifi'd he may arrive to the Honour of being the Warden, and then the Master of the Lodge, the Grand Warden, and at length the Grand Master of all the Lodges, according to his Merit.

No Brother can be a Warden until he has pass'd the part of a Fellow-Craft; nor a Master until he has acted as a Warden, nor Grand

Warden until he has been Master of a Lodge, nor Grand Master unless he has been a Fellow Craft before his Election, who is also to be nobly born, or a Gentleman of the best Fashion, or some eminent Scholar, or some curious Architect, or other Artist, descended of honest Parents, and who is of similar great Merit in the Opinion of the Lodges.

These Rulers and Governors, supreme and subordinate, of the ancient Lodge, are to be obey'd in their respective Stations by all the Brethren, according to the old Charges and Regulations, with all Humility, Reverence, Love and Alacrity.

V. Of the MANAGEMENT of the CRAFT in WORKING.

All Masons shall work honestly on Working Days, that they may live creditably on Holy Days; and the time appointed by the Law of the Land or confirm'd by Custom shall be observ'd. The most expert of the Fellow-Craftsmen shall be chosen or appointed the Master or Overseer of the Lord's Work; who is to be call'd Master by those that work under him. The Craftsmen are to avoid all ill Language, and to call each other by no disobliging Name, but Brother or Fellow; and to behave themselves courteously within and without the Lodge.

The Master, knowing himself to be able of Cunning, shall undertake the Lord's Work as reasonably as possible, and truly dispend his Goods as if they were his own; nor to give more Wages to any Brother or Apprentice than he really may deserve.

Both the Master and the Masons receiving their Wages justly, shall be faithful to the Lord and honestly finish their Work, whether Task or journey; nor put the work to Task that hath been accustomed to Journey.

None shall discover Envy at the Prosperity of a Brother, nor supplant him, or put him out of his Work, if he be capable to finish the same; for no man can finish another's Work so much to the Lord's Profit, unless he be thoroughly acquainted with the Designs and Draughts of him that began it.

When a Fellow-Craftsman is chosen Warden of the Work under the Master, he shall be true both to Master and Fellows, shall carefully oversee the Work in the Master's Absence to the Lord's profit; and his Brethren shall obey him.

All Masons employed shall meekly receive their Wages without Murmuring or Mutiny, and not desert the Master till the Work is finish'd.

A younger Brother shall be instructed in working, to prevent spoiling the Materials for want of Judgment, and for increasing and continuing of brotherly love.

All the Tools used in working shall be approved by the Grand Lodge.

No Labourer shall be employ'd in the proper Work of Masonry; nor shall Free Masons work with those that are not free, without an urgent Necessity; nor shall they teach Labourers and unaccepted Masons as they should teach a Brother or Fellow.

VI. Of BEHAVIOUR.

I. In the LODGE while CONSTITUTED.

You are not to hold private Committees, or separate Conversation without Leave from the Master, nor to talk of anything impertinent or unseemly, nor interrupt the Master or Wardens, or any Brother speaking to the Master: Nor behave yourself ludicrously or jestingly while the Lodge is engaged in what is serious and solemn; nor use any unbecoming Language upon any Pretense whatsoever; but to pay due Reverence to your Master, Wardens, and Fellows, and put them to Worship.

If any Complaint be brought, the Brother found guilty shall stand to the Award and Determination of the Lodge, who are the proper and competent Judges of all such Controversies (unless you carry it by Appeal to the Grand Lodge), and to whom they ought to be referr'd, unless a Lord's Work be hinder'd the meanwhile, in which Case a particular Reference may be made; but you must never go to Law about what concerneth Masonry, without an absolute necessity apparent to the Lodge.

2. BEHAVIOUR after the LODGE is over and the BRETHREN not GONE

You may enjoy yourself with innocent Mirth, treating one another according to Ability, but avoiding all Excess, or forcing any Brother to eat or drink beyond his Inclination, or hindering him from going when his Occasions call him, or doing or saying anything offensive, or that may forbid an easy and free Conversation, for that would blast our Harmony, and defeat our laudable Purposes. Therefore no private Piques or Quarrels must be brought within the Door of the Lodge, far less any Quarrels about Religion, or Nations, or State Policy, we being only, as Masons, of the Universal Religion above mention'd, we are also of all Nations, Tongues, Kindreds, and Languages, and are resolv'd against all Politics, as what never yet conduct'd to the Welfare of the Lodge, nor ever will.

3. BEHAVIOUR when BRETHREN meet WITHOUT STRANGERS, but not in a LODGE Formed.

You are to salute one another in a courteous Manner, as you will be instructed, calling each other Brother, freely giving mutual instruction as shall be thought expedient, without being ever seen or overheard, and without encroaching upon each other, or derogating from that Respect which is due to any Brother, were he not Mason: For though all Masons are as Brethren upon the same Level, yet Masonry takes no Honour from a man that he had before; nay, rather it adds to his Honour, especially if he has deserve well of the Brotherhood, who must give Honour to whom it is due, and avoid ill Manners.

4. BEHAVIOUR in presence of Strangers NOT MASONS.

You shall be cautious in your Words and Carriage, that the most penetrating Stranger shall not be able to discover or find out what is not proper to be intimated, and sometimes you shall divert a Discourse, and manage it prudently for the Honour of the worshipful Fraternity.

5. BEHAVIOUR at HOME, and in Your NEIGHBORHOOD.

You are to act as becomes a moral and wise Man; particularly not to let your Family, Friends and Neighbors know the Concern of the Lodge, &c., but wisely to consult your own Honour, and that of the ancient Brotherhood, for reasons not to be mention'd here You must also consult your Health, by not continuing together too late, or too long from Home, after Lodge Hours are past; and by avoiding of Gluttony or Drunkenness, that your Families be not neglected or injured, nor you disabled from working.

6. BEHAVIOUR toward a Strange BROTHER.

You are cautiously to examine him, in such a Method as Prudence shall direct you, that you may not be impos'd upon by an ignorant, false Pretender, whom you are to reject with contempt and Derision, and beware of giving him any Hints of Knowledge.

But if you discover him to be a true and genuine Brother, you are to respect him accordingly; and if he is in Want, you must relieve him if you can, or else direct him how he may be relieved; you must employ him some days, or else recommend him to be employ'd. But you are not charged to do beyond your ability, only to prefer a poor Brother, that is a good Man and true before any other poor People in the same Circumstance.

Finally, All these Charges you are to observe, and also those that shall be recommended to you in another Way; cultivating Brotherly Love, the Foundation and Cap-stone, the Cement and Glory of this Ancient Fraternity, avoiding all wrangling and quarreling, all Slander and Backbiting, nor permitting others to slander any honest Brother, but defending his Character, and doing him all good Offices, as far as is consistent with your Honour and Safety, and no farther. And if any of them do you Injury you must apply to your own or his Lodge, and from thence you may appeal to the Grand Lodge, at the Quarterly Communication and from thence to the annual Grand Lodge, as has been the ancient laudable Conduct but when the Case cannot be otherwise decided, and patiently listening to the honest and friendly Advice of Master and Fellows when they would prevent your going to Law with Strangers, or would excite you to put a speedy Period to all Lawsuits, so that you may mind the Affair of Masonry with the more Alacrity and Success; but with respect to Brothers or Fellows at Law, the Master and Brethren should kindly offer their Mediation, which ought to be thankfully submitted to by the contending Brethren; and if that submission is impracticable, they must, however, carry on their Process, or Lawsuit, without Wrath and Rancor (not In the common way) saying or doing nothing which may hinder Brotherly Love, and good Offices to be renew'd and continu'd; that all may see the benign Influence of Masonry, as all true Masons have done from the beginning of the World, and will do to the End of Time.

Amen, So Mote It Be

Thank you for buying this Cornerstone book!

For over 25 years now, we've tried to provide the Masonic community with quality books on Masonic education, philosophy, and general interest. Your support means everything to us and keeps us afloat. Cornerstone is by no means a large company. We are a small family owned operation that depends on your support.

Please visit our website and have a look at the many books we offer as well as the different categories of books.

If your lodge, Grand Lodge, research lodge, book club, or other body would like to have quality Cornerstone books to sell or distribute, write us. We can give you outstanding books, prices, and service.

Thanks again!

Cornerstone Book Publishers
1cornerstonebooks@gmail.com
http://cornerstonepublishers.com

www.ingramcontent.com/pod-product-compliance
Lightning Source LLC
Chambersburg PA
CBHW020420010526
44118CB00010B/350